GW00320402

Cont

MARKETING

John Stapleton completed his full time education at the University of Aston in Birmingham, and has had a varied in-depth career in marketing management. He has had experience as a salesman, sales manager, market research manager, marketing manager, and as a senior lecturer in advertising, media and statistics. He has worked in the printing, pharmaceuticals, telecommunications, detergents, construction, publishing and computer industries for British, American and European companies, large and small. He has written a number of books on marketing.

Mr Stapleton is a recipient of the Lord Mayor of London's Marketing Award, a Queen's Award to Industry and has appeared in the British High Court as an authority on marketing. Since 1969 he has been an independent consultant, and provides diagnostic and monitoring services into company marketing plans, advertising campaigns, and new product promotions.

TEACH YOURSELF BOOKS

MARKETING

John Stapleton

TEACH YOURSELF BOOKS

Hodder and Stoughton

First published 1975
Second edition 1984
Fourth impression 1988

Copyright © 1975, 1984
John Stapleton

British Library Cataloguing in Publication Data
Stapleton, John
Marketing.—2nd ed.—(Teach yourself books)
1. Marketing
I. Title
658.8   HF5415

ISBN 0 340 33920 9

Printed and bound in Great Britain for
Hodder and Stoughton Educational,
a division of Hodder and Stoughton Ltd,
Mill Road, Dunton Green, Sevenoaks, Kent,
by Richard Clay (The Chaucer Press) Ltd, Bungay, Suffolk
Photoset by Rowland Phototypesetting Ltd
Bury St Edmunds, Suffolk

Directing the sales effort. Monitoring the sales effort. Harmonising the sales effort. Field sales supervision.

Company service strategy. Credit control, allowances, returns, discounts, cancellations. Hire purchase, credit sales, leasing, factoring, franchising. After-sales service: installation, maintenance, service, spare parts. Customer guarantees and legal controls. Stock control. Telephone selling. Premiums and joint ventures. The sales office organisation. Enquiry handling. The sales supporting service. Management information, accounting, computers, operational research.

Gratification via the mass media. Characteristics of the behavioural sciences. Classification of population groups.

The brand manager. Product differentiation. Product policy. The marketing mix.

Operational checklist. A guide to quantitative analysis. Operational analysis. Planning considerations. The economic market. The market information system.

Preface

The needs of the marketing student have changed almost beyond recognition since the first edition of this book was published. Many of the early principles of marketing have become so widespread that they are now almost established practice. Successive governments, the media, and such diverse individual bodies as trade unions, professional entertainers and the armed forces refer to their professionalism and issue statements loaded with ideas once exclusive to people in the marketing business, and many of the early principles are now considered a matter of commonsense. So today's student approaches his or her course with an almost unrecognised body of marketing knowledge.

This edition acknowledges the changed market situation. It retains the basic principles so that a formal course of study for first-level examinations set by bodies such as the Institute of Marketing, the CAM Foundation, and the London Chamber of Commerce and Industry may be followed. In addition, it provides further details of those areas where rapid development has occurred – such as the behavioural approach, brand management and the use of the marketing mix – together with new chapters on case study analysis and quantitative techniques. Case study analysis, in particular, has become a major feature of all marketing courses, yet this is barely recognised in other books which are currently available.

My thanks are owed to my wife and partner Eileen Stapleton, whose work at The Marketing Tuition Centre, our jointly run marketing education centre, has made it possible for me to update the books on marketing that bear my name.

John Stapleton

1

Introduction to Marketing

Successful marketing actions are the result of management information and of applied common sense. Prosperous marketing companies are those that think positively about their business environment, so developing an organisation capable of seeking opportunity, recognising potential and resolving its difficulties. Although marketing techniques are still developing they are becoming increasingly scientific. The artistic qualities once attributed to marketing, mainly by uncomprehending practitioners, are decreasing rapidly in significance and recognition. In many ways this is unfortunate, as much of the inspiration for marketing has come from individual flair. Creativity still exists in advertising copy, design, and layout, however, much of it increasingly influenced by the behavioural sciences.

The word marketing is often equated with what was once called *sales management* but which, since the development of trading, has been known as *distribution*. 'Marketing' is not a synonym for these terms but denotes the wider understanding and greater complexity which have become common in recent years. Before the Industrial Revolution tradesmen produced goods in small quantities for sale in their own close-knit communities. With the increasing availability of machinery it became possible, and indeed necessary, to increase production to pay for the cost of the equipment. Local demand was limited and, although there was some stimulation, it became necessary for the tradesmen to travel to other communities in search of orders.

Constant development and improvement of manufacturing processes has made even larger markets necessary. As markets have grown and production increased, the unit cost of each item manufactured has declined in real terms. Whereas there was a time when only wealthy people could afford most commodities, the reduction in unit cost and increased earnings by consumers have resulted in more and more being bought by the greater part of the population. Effectively, even local markets have shown considerable expansion.

During most of this early industrial period there was no way by which the customer could identify the manufacturer. He would select the goods he required according to his own knowledge and experience. Many goods made available by unscrupulous tradesmen were of a low standard and, in an effort to protect the growth of their industry, suppliers began to put their own names on the goods they produced, indicating to the public that the goods bearing their name would be of an acceptable quality and good value for money. With branding established, manufacturers and tradesmen realised the opportunities for promoting the sale of their own products. Thus publicity and selling techniques, as we know them today, were developed.

Immediately after the end of the Second World War consumer demand was almost insatiable. After many years of being deprived of many of the necessities and comforts of life the public was eager to obtain whatever products it could find. For several years almost every article produced could have been sold many times over. During this period promotional techniques were almost unnecessary. They were only used as a means of informing the public that the manufacturer's goods were now available and where they could be obtained. Gradually this sellers' market eased and firms that had enjoyed constant pressure of demand found that not only were alternative sources of supply established but also consumers were becoming more discriminating in their choice. Quality standards had to be improved. As more and more consumers' demands were satisfied, manufacturers found that they had to develop new markets in order to survive. Once again it became necessary to stimulate demand, not only overseas but also to expand the total market at home.

Faced with a discerning market, manufacturers raised quality standards, redesigned or reformulated products to meet more discriminating tastes, raised the standard of informative literature and emphasised the tangible benefits that their product had over their competitors'. They made it convenient for consumers to purchase by improving distribution facilities and providing satisfactory after-sales service. The need for marketing techniques had returned. Now much market activity is devoted to brand-switching, with pure market development a comparative rarity.

Many non-marketing executives question the validity of marketing expenditure. Marketing activities are the creative element of business activity. They are the means by which the company's income is obtained. They are an integral part of the business and should be considered as much a part of the cost of supply as the productive process itself. Without marketing expenditure there would be no sales; production would be unnecessary. Marketing expenditure for most businesses results in a level of pricing that could not be achieved without modern marketing techniques.

Machine-made shoes conforming to popular taste are made by the thousand at a production cost that may be only a few pence. In making the shoes available in the quantities demanded, the manufacturer is obliged to contribute towards the operating costs and the profit of a wholesaler, who in turn distributes the shoes to retailers, who will also incur operating costs and need to make a profit. Under such circumstances the distribution costs may seem out of all proportion to the manufacturing costs. By comparison, a pair of hand-made shoes selling at, perhaps, two or three times the price of machine-made shoes will have high production costs and distribution costs may be small – just sufficient to pay for the shop at which the cobbler works. In most cases the machine-made shoes will appear to be better value for money to the vast majority of consumers. The purchaser of hand-made shoes will have some special requirement for which he is prepared to pay a higher price. In comparing the two, the marketing costs of machine-made shoes are justified by the effect they have had on the final selling price. Certainly as far as the consumer is concerned, the division between manufacturing and marketing is of little consequence so long as the final price is low.

Distribution costs have also increased as a direct wish of the consumer expressed through demand in the market place. Consumers have shown themselves willing to pay premium prices for products that carry *added value* in convenience. Frozen foods and packaged goods provide this added convenience and consumers pay the additional charges incurred in distributing these goods. Previously consumers had to pay for these processes – not in money but in the time spent in preparing the products for consumption. Many costs of distribution borne by industry are eventually paid for by the consumer to ensure that he or she maintains a freedom of choice, a freedom to buy on credit and the freedom that comes as a result of the educational efforts made by industry and commerce. Hire purchase and credit sales incur additional costs borne by consumers in order to benefit immediately from their purchases.

Part of the marketing process is devoted to reducing the cost of other marketing activities and to avoiding production waste; research for example, into channels and costs of distribution, promotional techniques and particularly development of products that consumers need. Henry Ford has long been acclaimed a pioneer of mass production. Yet it is clear from his autobiography that he was also a pioneer of the modern marketing philosophy. In *My Life and Work* he tells how he first found the price at which cars would sell by the million, then developed his production techniques accordingly. So by carrying out market research, he was helping to reduce production costs of cars. In the consumer field major changes in the distribution of products through self-service outlets and mail order concerns have reduced marketing costs. Packages, frozen foods, see-through containers, plastic bottles and jars, and bubble-packed items have all contributed to greater efficiency even in production. Services, such as building society branches, travel operators, insurance brokers, and money shops have all brought greater efficiency to the company. Many companies in their advertising now invite people to quote credit card numbers for payment of goods to be bought, and computer terminals are used to process orders and money at the point of purchase. So marketing helps to reduce costs in both production and distribution.

Substitutes have become a major feature in today's world where, for example, products made from the soya bean and new plastics are replacing traditional and expensive goods, and creating entirely new markets. This has introduced a new dimension to the concept of value.

Concepts in marketing

In order to understand marketing principles the non-marketing executive must become accustomed to entirely new concepts. To the professional marketer products are not just what they are but what they do. 'Selling the sizzle not the steak' is an expression frequently used to denote marketing theory. In persuading a consumer to buy a product for which a latent need has been established, a marketing-orientated company presents its goods in a way that will appeal to the consumers' needs. In emphasising benefits to the consumer, the seller is portraying his product in its best possible light and is helping the potential buyer to understand what the product will do for him; for example, in promoting a brand of petrol, the seller recognises the need for economical motoring and will emphasise the mileage that may be achieved through using his product. Other sellers may believe that the consumer is more interested in buying a product that not only fulfils its main purpose but will also satisfy psychological needs. The cosmetic manufacturer or the dressmaker will often concentrate promotional themes on the beauty the user can obtain in the same way that the pharmaceutical manufacturer will stress the health-giving qualities of his product – for both product groups help to instil confidence and hope in the user and so give him or her greater satisfaction from life. Equally, the industrial manufacturer may promote the idea of reduced worry rather than emphasise the increased efficiency that may be possible. This exemplifies the behavioural approach to marketing.

Such promotions are aimed at chosen groups of people, market segments, in an attempt to differentiate the brand concerned so as to give it a unique appeal. Segmentation and brand differentiation are essential principles in marketing. They are the means by which a company secures its competitive advantage.

Although often described as a promotional or a distributive activity, marketing is a function whose ultimate aim is to maximise profitability. It can best be described as a fundamental policy-forming activity devoted to selecting and developing suitable products for sale – promoting and distributing these products in a manner providing the optimum return on capital employed. As the optimum rate of profitability is usually achieved through high production runs, the greater the numbers of a particular product produced, the better the profit opportunity. In essence this means manufacturing the product that is likely to appeal to the majority of the population. The consumer still retains freedom of choice because smaller firms will concentrate their efforts on gaps left by the larger companies. Often the larger company will provide a wide choice by producing a basic product and providing many optional extras sufficient to appeal to the most extreme tastes. Although breadth of choice is still reduced, variety will always be maintained dependent upon demand. Thus choice is decided by the market.

The growth of marketing techniques in the twentieth century has been aided by parallel advances in international communications. International travel, worldwide tourism and the speed at which persons can move from one part of the world to another have created a 'shrinkage' in the size of the globe. Social, cultural and nationalistic barriers are being eliminated. The telephone, radio, television and space satellites have brought the nations of the world closer to each other, with greater understanding and tolerance towards historical differences. Such developments have made it easier for manufacturers to create worldwide mass markets for their products. This easing of communication has made it possible for educational and other influential actions to create a common acceptance for certain products. Bigger markets and increasing demand have required greater capitalisation for production and for the introduction of more economical manufacturing techniques.

The increasing complexity of products available and the ever-growing rate of technological progress have made it difficult for the average consumer to be knowledgeable when buying goods. Manufacturers make use of marketing activities to make available to purchasers the necessary information. Advertising campaigns and descriptive literature are intended to make available the information a consumer requires to decide for himself the product most suitable for his needs. Manufacturers are not expected to be impartial in the information they provide. Each manufacturer has made a product which he feels is most suitable for the market and he will always emphasise the most important features in his promotional activities. He could not – nor could he be expected to – provide information on product qualities which he believes are unnecessary and which he has chosen not to include in his own product. To make a satisfactory purchase the consumer must obtain information from competing manufacturers and decide for himself which particular products and specific benefits he seeks from the range concerned. Often the consumer will decide in favour of a well-known and well-established manufacturer in whom he is able to place some confidence because of the company's name and past reputation. He may make this decision irrespective of the competing values of the products concerned. Consumer organisations such as the Consumers Association, the publishers of *Which?*, help in this process by accelerating the effect that differentials in the market place would achieve.

Although many people still dispute the validity of marketing practices in a business enterprise, it is reasonable to assume that a wise businessman would not make continually increasing investment in marketing unless he were convinced that he was getting value for money. Marketing activities are not yet exactly quantifiable, but more and more efforts are being made to develop marketing into a more exact science. At this stage it is possible to apply logical deductions by observation, in a general assessment of marketing effectiveness. By carefully assembling market information, management is able to reduce business risk by the elimination of non-influencing data, thus improving general economic prosperity. Planning future requirements carefully in each stage of the distribution process enables a company to avoid unnecessary expenditure in misdirected and ineffective investment. By setting sales targets and developing marketing strategy to achieve these targets the company creates effective new markets among existing and new customers. Developing better understanding of customer needs enables a company to improve its communication processes. It can provide better information and services for these customers, thus creating additional goodwill among the many organisations involved in its day-to-day operations.

In any business environment there will always be an infinite number of variables which are often in conflict. Applied marketing techniques help to reduce the number of such variables and to channel company resources towards maximising profits and minimising costs according to short-, medium- or long-term needs. In the struggle to win more profitable sales a company may make use of a wide variety of specialist skills. It is in selecting and coordinating these skills that the marketing function is seen to perform its most obvious role. The marketing mix, as this permutation is known, is based on the requirements in the market place, provided that these needs are sufficient in volume to attract the attention of the company concerned.

Definitions of marketing

Numerous definitions of marketing have been suggested by any number of learned authorities, companies and writers. In some cases the emphasis has been on the concept of marketing, in others on the activities of marketing. It is clear that the two are interdependent, yet where the concept is understood the activities are a natural consequence. Where the concept is not understood, then the activities may be misdirected and ineffective.

Some companies may indicate that despite the non-existence of a marketing department they have still been successful. This does not mean that the company has not been marketing orientated, for the executives concerned may be fully aware of the concept of marketing and may practise its principles without giving title to the functions involved. It is, however, unfortunately still common for a company to appoint marketing executives and yet not understand the basic requirements of the marketing function. Certainly the activities of marketing seem clear, for they will normally include the promotional activities of the company along with the required ancillary services. The marketing concept is less definite but more fundamental to business success. It is a management philosophy, an attitude of mind, to which the complete involvement of every company executive and employee is necessary, and in which the entire operation of the company is devoted towards the satisfaction of consumer needs. The definition adopted by the Institute of Marketing is as follows:

> 'Marketing is the management process responsible for identifying, anticipating and satisfying customer requirements profitably.'

There is no doubt from this definition that the Institute clearly recognises the management philosophy of marketing and that successful companies are those that adopt this philosophy at all levels. In a modern company no functional executive, or white- or blue-collar worker, is without some direct or indirect contact with the firm's markets. The attitudes of the chief executive will be communicated via the staff to customers. The floor sweeper in the factory will have an effect on the customers in the way that he performs his tasks in keeping dust from, say, precision machinery or food vats. Every employee in searching for a new job is conveying impressions of his employers to everyone who sees him and has a need for his particular skill. No individual in today's company should, therefore, lack motivation in marketing understanding.

In normal circumstances the primary contact which management takes as priority is with customers. Not only is this concept critical but even the practice of marketing involves other functional activities, for all commercial functions have some sort of customer contact. It is for this reason that marketing direction overlaps into other business functions.

Marketing, however, is a multi-dimensional, global term used by different industries to describe how they tackle their various problems in the market place. One essential distinction is between cosmetic marketing and diagnostic marketing. *Cosmetic* marketing is the recognisable part, comprising communications by advertising, selling and public relations. *Diagnostic* marketing is the investigative and planning part that is not easily recognisable, but which determines and limits the cosmetic approach. Some companies seem unaware of the need for diagnostic work and seek communications solutions to their problems. This, metaphorically, is selecting a rifle without considering the target, the cost of the ammunition and the problems of hunting. A profitable outcome will owe more to chance than judgment.

The entrepreneur in marketing

All commercial activities are created to provide goods or services. During their evolution many firms expand their activities, often with new products and new markets. At the time of creation the entrepreneur usually tries to meet an existing need rather than to stimulate a new demand or highlight an unconscious one.

Normally he will have established connections, a specific skill or knowledge and an awareness of the requirements of his potential customers. At this time his business activity is probably clear and he is unlikely to have felt the need to consider fully the scope of his operations or to formulate his operational problems in depth. But this is not always the case where the entrepreneur concerned has already had extensive managerial experience. An example from industry is provided by Midcast Numerical Control (Wales) Ltd. The managing director saw a requirement for an expert organisation totally committed to the application of numerical control systems. So he set up a team operating in small premises in Leicester where he had daily access to any part of the country and where there was an abundance of skilled engineering labour. His company and its associates were pioneers of the use of numerical control as the technological Esperanto of Europe, since numerical control dismisses the main difficulty of international collaboration – the language barrier among engineers and technicians.

In the industry facing Midcast the ideal marketing pitch was technical competence. So the company saw its opportunity, knew its market and, because it had always kept its finger on the pulse, was able to organise almost from the start the full range of services, a programming package, necessary for sound growth.

Established companies, on the other hand, operating in a mixture of growing, static or declining markets, and who need to reappraise their business functions regularly and to assess their future prospects for survival, regrettably do not seem to practise the same discipline. Often failure to do so may result in lost market share, product obsolescence, redundancies or even bankruptcy.

Acceptance of marketing principles and the use of marketing techniques have sometimes been forced on companies by competitive pressures in the market place. In an effort to stimulate demand for their own brands, manufacturers seek product innovation and attempt to improve the effectiveness of their operations by researching and developing the needs of consumers. Industrial companies have been slower to adopt marketing techniques, for their production, in unit terms, has been relatively small and their number of customers comparatively low. They do not often achieve a dominant market share and any contraction in immediate purchasing levels is spread evenly over the larger part of the market. Industrial companies also tend to be more widely diversified in their product range, and a depression in one industry may be compensated in another. Because of their size such companies tend to be more flexible and can adjust to lower production rates more readily.

One could well argue that the adoption of marketing techniques by industrial companies has been forced on them by stagnant national economies and competition from the whole of manufacturing industry for the limited capital investment available. In this sense typewriters are competing against carpets for the industrial buyers' money.

Service industries

Few of the service industries have yet felt the pressure of competitive forces with sufficient intensity for the practice of marketing to have been widely adopted. True, retail stores are more market conscious now that other methods of serving the customer have been developed. In the insurance market, companies have had to become market orientated. Traditionally a selling operation, insurance companies have had to develop more sophisticated selling techniques and to look at the problems of the buyer. The emphasis is now on insurance as a pension medium, due to income tax advantages, rather than as a security arrangement. Once again marketing adoption has come from competition – from unit trusts. The competition has forced a substantial increase in the total market, a frequent result of marketing usage.

Until the breakdown of the tariff agreement between insurance companies, active competition was restricted. It is such restrictive practices that have delayed the development of marketing techniques in many service industries. These contain a large element of professional men practising rules of conduct imposed by collective agreement among members of the appropriate association. There are over 150 such professional bodies in the UK, with hundreds of thousands of members.

Members may not be allowed to advertise, they are often forbidden to obtain business by pricing concessions, and they must not endeavour to sell or promote their business in the generally accepted way. The sole means by which they expect to win new business is by recommendation. Professional bodies believe that these agreements are in the public interest and that they help to maintain minimum standards of competence.

The United Kingdom's Monopolies Commission in its 1970 report did not agree. The Commission said that the agreements were a restraint on the improvement of efficiency and tended to protect the incompetent. The Commission recommended the abolition of all such restrictive practices, leaving the way clear for the introduction of marketing activities by the more progressive organisations. Since that time some solicitors' firms have undertaken promotional activity but, in the main, marketing actions have been taken by institutions representing each of the professions.

The banking profession has suffered at the hands of successive governments through restrictions on the use of its basic product – by squeeze and by freeze. In return for the cooperation of the banking movement Parliament produced its own banking-type operation – the National Giro – and then allowed it advantages that had been withheld from the banking system. In facing this competition and in overcoming the restrictions to growth from which it had suffered for so long, the banking profession adopted marketing attitudes and practices at a speed that would delight many a hardened marketing protagonist. In consequence, the National Giro in facing the new initiative failed to achieve its original objectives.

In recent years the banking business has developed positive and realistic approaches to marketing: advertising in the mass media using appealing slogans, face-lifts in its branches, after-hours cash-dispensing facilities, promotions to students, and the beginnings of a return to Saturday opening. To varying degrees the banks have become marketing orientated.

International marketing

Competition at home has forced many companies to search overseas for outlets. In order to exploit the best of its opportunities, the forward-looking company will increase its sales abroad so as to maximise profit potential. Modern management does not operate in an atmosphere conducive to selling internationally – or so it seems. This attitude is inconsistent with the concept of marketing, which does not differentiate between groups of people by region. Markets are divided by need or by application of a product which satisfies that need. Marketing opportunities exist wherever there are people, and the fact that these people may be separated by political, cultural or social differences does not necessarily diminish the degree of opportunity. These differences may only influence the way in which the opportunity is seized.

It is necessary first to evaluate the existing opportunities and then to plan to satisfy those showing signs of producing the best results. By assessing the most common needs throughout the globe, and in particular those indicating a future substantial growth rate, and by developing the product which best satisfies that need, the company will not only be adopting the best current marketing practice but will also be well on the way to successful overseas development.

Principles of marketing

An understanding of the true nature of marketing has been shown by Roy Jenkins, managing director of Quantum Sciences Ltd, who explains:

'At one extreme end of marketing-orientated units is the market-orientated company. Such an organisation sets up a selling machine designed to operate in one or more clearly defined market places. It operates by feeding to this machine products of any description which can be sold economically in the chosen markets. It maximises the efficiency of the selling machine by multiplying the opportunities to make sales from a wide product range without significantly increasing calling or other costs. The market-orientated company accepts no short-term flexibility in choice of the market but complete flexibility in terms of supply.

'At the other extreme is the product or production-orientated company. It is usual to think of this type of organisation as being the opposite of marketing-orientated but this is not necessarily so. This sort of unit can still use marketing techniques.

'The product or production-orientated organisation is tied by materials or technical equipment or people to a narrow band of products. Whatever field it operates in it is essentially a "quarry". It cannot profitably move on to a new "hole" until it has earned enough profits to be able to abandon the old one. However, it does have complete flexibility in its choice of markets and selling methods. The move of the brewers into production of antibiotics is an obvious example of the utilisation of existing production methods to match the needs of a new market. Most of the famous names in fine china with large investments in clay mines and plant are now earning the bulk of their profits from industrial ceramics. In the early 1950s the author took a small photographic and block-making outfit and moved into the new field of electronics printed production without spending a penny on new plant.'

Often the framework within which the company decides to operate comes as a result of segmentation, or gap analysis as it is often termed. The process of segmentation may be through markets, products, geographical areas, or psychographical distinctions. Usually the term is associated with markets. Spotting a gap in a market, seeing a need and providing the means by which that need is satisfied portrays the commonly accepted version of the marketing entrepreneur. And it is this vision – sighting an opportunity, seizing it and devoting one's entire existence to its success – that is the predominant feature of *market segmentation*. Such an example is provided by Norman Fletcher (Sales and Developments) Ltd.

In 1960 Norman Fletcher, a West Bromwich shop-owner and life-long boating enthusiast, set about designing a boat. After much trial and error he finally developed his own glassfibre design. He wasted no time in putting it to the ultimate test – on the water. It attracted much immediate attention and comment. Knowing the boating fraternity well, he backed his own judgment and began manufacturing replicas on a small scale. Soon after he sold a boat to Ray Potter, a notable racing enthusiast, who promptly expressed his satisfaction in his new acquisition by offering to join Norman in his enterprise. They both knew that crowded roads were frustrating people's drive for speed and excitement. The comparative safety of boat and sea, and the tranquillity away from crowds were bound to catch on.

An example of *product segmentation* is given by Morgan Adhesives of Canada, where through advanced technology the company has developed adhesives suitable for pressure application with paper, foils and vinyls. Using this highly flexible and multi-purpose product the company has been able to develop business applications for use in a wide range of industries.

For *geographical segmentation* we can consider the Fife Forge Co. Ltd of Kirkcaldy in Scotland. Although 100 years old, the company made a major change in its policy in 1963, when it began the gradual introduction of a young management team, revised its entire marketing strategy and developed a modernisation programme for its production facilities. The gradual decline of the shipbuilding industry in the UK required the company to seek markets elsewhere. The new management team decided to explore opportunities in markets, especially in the underdeveloped countries, where indigenous forges did not exist. By carrying out market research into the world shipbuilding industry, several likely countries were selected and in-depth investigations were started to establish the requirements in each particular country. The company succeeded primarily by selecting geographical market segments.

A classic example of psychographical distinction is the slogan "Put a tiger in your tank". The campaign attracted a considerable amount of business away from petroleum competitors although the product had no material advantage over competition. Such appeals to people's deep-rooted emotions are now common in marketing communications.

These examples demonstrate the principles of segmentation which continue to have wide application to the provision of goods and services alike. Recent parallels are McCain Oven Chips, Natrena Sweetners, microwave ovens and home video recorders in market segmentation; and instant-bond glues, digital alarm watches and plastic car bumpers in product segmentation. Examples of geographical segmentation include construction development in the Middle East, engineering projects in Nigeria and banking in South America. Psychographical examples are Persil Soap Powder, Birds Eye Peas, Oxo Meat Extract, Mum Deodorant, and Virgin Records.

Many manufacturers make the mistake of trying to offer a full range for a particular model in a new market. This may work for a car manufacturer, where servicing facilities are critical to sales, but usually it is more practical to enter the market with one product showing promise, establish the company's name among consumers and distributors, and later widen the range as the demand justifies.

If a marketing man accepts the principle that there is scope in any business depending on the way he goes about it, and studies his market, his product and his operational methods, he will probably find that he has become a pioneer in his industry. The most startling innovations have come from men who have looked at industries operating without significant change over many years and who plugged the gaps they found.

Distribution and marketing

Frequently traditional business practices work against the new-comer. Competing on equal terms is often impossible. Established companies not only have the confidence of the trade but, in order to protect their vested interests, they may often make deliberate efforts to deter new entrants. One of the major justifications for the massive advertising campaigns between the detergents giants was to make it impossible for other companies to break into the market.

A Monopolies Commission report did not support this attitude, yet when unbranded equivalents appeared alongside their branded alternatives they did not sell. The market seemed unconvinced. However, within the last few years some manufacturers have produced equivalents to branded goods, dispensed with promotion and sold through established outlets alongside both branded goods and own–label products. The sales growth of these generics, as they have been called, has been encouraging. Their success supports the view that mass advertising prohibits the success of new brands, yet also defeats the argument because these generics *are* sometimes branded, with a reputation for economy. But this is marketing. One practice fails, but changing market conditions enable the same practice to succeed. Inflation and unemployment have forced economy on many, to the point where a new social grade is emerging within the socioeconomic class structure.

The retail trade has recognised the pressures on its customers. Stocks of pasta-type products and substitute foods with soya bean and adulterated meat composition have appeared for the mass markets, alongside wider ranges of cheeses, fish and meats for the more affluent. Offering such goods, along with own–labels and the generics, emphasises the retailers' aim to promote outlet loyalty rather than the brand loyalty sought by manufacturers.

Sometimes the trade will oppose a new product, no matter how superior it may be, unless the promoter can advertise at a level that will ensure sales exceeding those of the existing product. Often the companies that try innovation stimulate the total market and a more substantial market results – to the benefit of all.

Meanwhile suppliers unable to break into the established distribution network, together with those trying to stimulate new growth alongside this network, are moving into direct marketing. They may try to service their target audiences themselves or they may adopt an alternative distribution network using direct response or mail order supply methods.

2

The Practice of Marketing

In a modern emancipated society the individual is allowed a measure of free will and choice and is allowed to make his own decisions, whether they be right or wrong for him. In allowing these freedoms there must be competition for his preferences, and a drive for resultant profits is tolerable. This is the basis upon which our society lives and expands.

It contrasts with a totalitarian state operating a planned economy, where some official decides on behalf of the population what its tastes should be, what is good for it and how it should spend its money. In such a society there is no universal demand for marketing practices, although some of its activities exist in other forms, such as propaganda.

Marketing is an integral part of the business operation. It is the fundamental by which industry sells its products. To curtail marketing or to eliminate it altogether would be like suggesting that industry should stop selling – a process that would remove the dynamic element in the national economy and hence diminish the growth rate in both production and job opportunity. In some industries, such as office equipment or data processing, it would be more than the growth rate that would suffer. In the new industries, selling to new markets is essential, and in the modernised production plants of the established industries marketing effort is necessary to achieve the volume essential in maintaining low unit costs and remaining competitive internationally. So marketing provides the stimulus upon which economic progress is based. Without it modern industry tends to stagnate, for it is marketing practice that makes improvements in productivity possible and so gives society the improved standard of living it constantly demands. In *The Wealth of Nations*, Adam Smith wrote: 'Consumption is the sole end and purpose of all production; and the interest of the producer ought to be attended to only so far as it may be necessary for promoting that of the consumer.'

In the UK during the 1980s the introduction of Channel 4, breakfast television, teletext, and the extension of independent local radio have provided the marketing communications opportunities for many medium-sized firms. Cable television has been the subject of experiment in some areas, such as Milton Keynes, and following the Hunt Committee Report in 1983 is likely to further extend the opportunities for more firms. Not only do these new communications facilities provide for market expansion by the smaller firms, but for test marketing by larger firms.

The most criticised activity of marketing is advertising. Salesmanship has always been the subject of dispute, but it is always possible for consumers to take refuge from its practitioners. Not so with advertising, for that is partly the secret of its success. Advertisements appear in the morning mail, on every form of transport, are widespread in leisure pursuits and follow the family into the home at night via the television screen; advertising is therefore complementary to selling. There are some who believe the sole purpose of advertising is to inform. This is inaccurate. Advertising is intended to inform in order to sell. It sells by informing people in as persuasive a way as possible. It emphasises the benefits that the manufacturer develops in his product so that the consumer might buy. The advertiser describes his product as being the best there is because he believes this to be true. And it is – for his chosen market. He has spent time researching the market place and establishing people's needs, and has then developed a product accordingly. Following this he goes out into the market place and promotes the product he has specially developed for the market he has selected. For people in that market his product is the best value for money available. So the manufacturer will not normally give information on the limitations inherent in his product or, generally speaking, on applications for which the product is unsuitable. Nor should he be expected to. The features he believes necessary are included and the appropriate applications indicated; anything else has been left out as unwarranted. He cannot be held responsible for the wishful thinking of consumers – the hope that their £1 will buy a product worth £5. So in marketing terms the manufacturer will have selected a group of people as his market, and he provides the appropriate product most suitable for them. He cannot in all fairness be expected to give details of facilities he considers unnecessary and be responsible for and to people for whom the product has not been made. People who accuse manufacturers of misleading practices are often guilty of their own inability or disinclination to study and compare the available alternatives.

Reputable manufacturers have never been a problem, for they have established policies that are customer-orientated. The principles underlying these policies have been adopted by legislators and appear under Fair Trading and other Acts, while codes of practice are followed by those firms who are members of professional bodies.

How marketing benefits society

Marketing is practised in every country where goods are in abundance. But production alone does not create wealth. Wealth comes from *selling* goods, not from simply producing them; ask any businessman left with a warehouse full of unsaleable goods. Equally, any emphasis on increasing productivity is inadequate without a parallel increase in consumption. Producing more goods per worker implies more sales needed per worker and, logically, more consumption to absorb the extra produce. You cannot increase the wealth of the nation without raising consumption and that requires marketing. Production is a poor second, for wealth can be improved *without raising the level of production*. Increasing prices alone will suffice but only in the short term.

The principal benefits of marketing to society are:

1 Lowering of prices
2 Improving quality
3 Reducing business risk
4 Aiding technological progress
5 Subsidising education and leisure
6 Reducing cognitive dissonance
7 Providing jobs

8 Creating consumer choice
9 International trade
10 Social marketing.

These factors all contribute to improving the standard of living of the nation, and in many ways perform the socialistic doctrine of more for everyone. The way in which this is achieved is complex but the philosophy is simple. Consider the factors closely:

1 Lowering of prices

All economists agree on the principle of the economies of scale. Some may question its truth in practice, but all agree that it is possible and often achievable. Certainly the unit-cost price of a product is reduced after mass markets have been opened. Not all achieve dramatic reductions in price, for many reductions are almost indiscernible. Women's tights, prior to mini-skirts, were used generally by entertainers and sports personalities. Today, in real terms, prices are a small fraction of original costs, and tights sell by the million instead of by the thousand. But most products take many years to reach high volume sales and reduction in costs prices are achieved quite slowly. So instead of introducing actual price reductions, manufacturers tend to absorb many cost increases and raise selling prices at a rate much lower than inflation would suggest. Therefore in real terms prices are falling relative to increases in purchasing power.

2 Improving quality

In the earlier part of the century competing goods were largely homogeneous and not distinguishable one from the other. But with the advancement of advertising, manufacturers started to put their name on their product and branding spread. So in competition for the purchasers' money, manufacturers struggled to improve the quality of their output. Sometimes this would be by the reformulation of a product and sometimes by repackaging or even redesigning the product to make it more acceptable. In this way frozen foods or instant mixes are considered improvements in quality.

3 Reducing business risk

Although this may seem primarily to the benefit of the capitalist, it does nonetheless bring considerable benefits to society. Marketing helps to improve the quality of business decisions, and that can mean avoidance of waste of resources and less likelihood of business failure and unemployment.

It also implies more confidence in the taking of risks, and hence the whole of society benefits from the extra product choices thus made available.

4 Aiding technological progress
In the struggle to prosper, or even survive, firms must innovate – not just in commercial practices but in products themselves. It is modern marketing that has enabled products such as Xerography, ballpoint pens, colour television and the like to become readily available to those who want them. Technological progress rarely comes from the scientist working outside commercial pressures. The only commercial technological spin-off from the American space programme was non-stick frying pans. Yet commercially there have been many new ideas, ranging from moon-walk toys to telephone operator mouthpieces.

5 Subsidising education and leisure
Neither the newspaper industry nor commercial television could survive today without marketing subsidies. Newspapers rely on advertising revenue for the larger part of their income, while commercial television is dependent entirely on the advertisers' money. These two media account for the most significant proportion of after-school education, whether it be cultural, academic, scientific, moral, religious, artistic or whatever. Advertisers also support most of the leisure pursuits; because they want to appeal *en masse* they tend to spend their money where people gather together, at sports grounds, etc. Furthermore, advertisers support such activities as round the world voyages, beauty competitions and man's flamboyant struggle against the elements. So modern life would be inconceivable without marketing influences.

6 Reducing cognitive dissonance
All buyers are wary of making a mistake, for no one can be an expert on all things. But well-promoted goods offered by well-known companies with such policies as sale on approval, sale or return, or

after-sales services provide reassurance. In this way consumers are relieved of anxiety. They will be able to buy relatively expensive items confident of the quality and assured of service and attention should something be wrong.

7   Providing jobs
Higher levels of demand brought by marketing necessitate distribution channels and physical distribution facilities. As such, the infrastructure of the nation involving ports, roads, motorways, ships, trucks, trains, airports, and telecommunication networks becomes critical and the provision of these services brings jobs to millions.

8   Creating consumer choice
Competition and the need to achieve a return on investment compels firms continually to extend their product range. Consumers are provided with a full choice, sufficient to satisfy all but the most difficult tastes.

9   International trade
Marketing skills applied to overseas countries stimulate demand in those countries and so develop trade. The UK imports most of its food and must pay for it through the sales of manufactured items and capital goods, and invisible earnings. The standard of living in most countries of the world is now dependent on the ability of each country to export its goods and services.

10   Social marketing
Many companies now seek to ensure that their commercial and industrial activities are seen to be responsive to the needs and concerns of society. Similarly, politicians, trade unions, government departments, charities and community service organisations use marketing techniques to promote their ideas and services to the community in an attempt to disseminate information which they consider beneficial or leading to greater awareness of the help available. In some cases the information provided is intended to make more people aware of the plight of others less fortunate.

By the judicial use of its marketing funds, today's company makes it possible for almost everyone to share the fruits of progress. Although the initial, often extravagant quality sometimes suffers, and complaints come most frequently from those able to disregard the price tag, it is considered better for everyone to enjoy a mediocre product mass-produced than for the majority to go without altogether. It would not be extreme to say that improvements in the standard of living achieved this century by advanced nations are largely attributable to marketing and the influence it has had in the allocation of productive resources. One could say almost that capitalism has been achieving the aims of socialism.

In the 1980s marketing action is arguably the only means to bring about an early return to full employment, by stimulating demand, increasing consumption and bringing demand for both labour and capital. The government's role may be to provide more generous tax allowances against marketing expenditure, as is accepted in other aspects of business. Such allowances would prove to be a sound investment for governments because successful firms pay more taxes than those which only just survive.

The marketing family tree

Marketing is still the subject of much misunderstanding, for it is not just the prodigy of the twentieth century but a whole family of prodigies. The father goes back many centuries to the beginning of trading, when merchants recognised the need to obtain the foods people craved for rather than products that might have been just food for their souls. The mother is a phenomenon of the nineteenth and twentieth centuries. Using the fast-developing network of communication systems, the 'activities of marketing', the so-called marketing mix, joined with the ancient 'concept of marketing' and spawned the family of today. Moreover, it is the confusion in identifying the offspring that antagonises most non-marketing executives. For although they spring from the same seed and believe in the same philosophies, the branches of the marketing family tree have reached different degrees of maturity and, like all children, have formed their own unique characteristics. So the practice of marketing in each branch of the family shows a markedly different profile. The branches are:

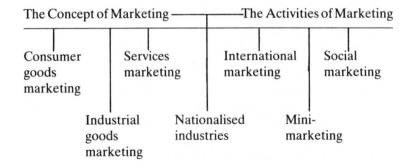

Each of these areas of marketing practice has used the principle or principles most applicable to its own market – true market orientation, and developed it to the point where it may almost dominate marketing management. Thus in consumer goods marketing, where adequate distribution is sought by the use of *advertising pull* – getting consumers to seek and ask for the product by name – marketing is almost synonymous with advertising; certainly the marketing manager or brand manager will be an advertising man, probably with agency experience. Similarly, in industrial goods marketing, where outlets are comparatively few, the most significant activity is selling – the winning of confidence – and the top marketing job will be filled by a former salesman, almost invariably from the same industry, since established contact is almost invaluable – *sales push*.

Consumer goods marketing

In the early days of established trading practices the manufacturer had to depend on merchants to carry his goods far and wide for sale in provincial or colonial market towns. Bartering was common and dishonesty in trade an accepted practice. Goods were degraded and suppliers paid with debased coin. So in order to prosper and grow a manufacturer had to find a distribution network that gave honesty and reliability. The tied-house system in public houses is probably attributable to this need. Door-to-door selling, as practised by pedlars, was the only alternative to the merchants selling at the village markets, so chaos was assured. The image left by these traders lingers on in society's view of selling and salesmanship.

But the consumer goods industry was rescued, not by the trade channels but by a collection of consumers. For manufacturers were not the only ones to suffer from dishonest traders; the customers themselves resisted any extension of the practice by setting up their own retail outlets with goods manufactured under the control of the retailer – the birth of the co-operative movement. Within ten years the pioneers of Rochdale launched the Co-operative Wholesale Society, in 1855, to supply the branches that had been opened. By the end of the century multiple traders in the UK, such as Liptons and Home & Colonial, had opened hundreds of branches in competition with the Co-op. So the mass marketing of foods hitherto the province of the affluent, such as flour, tea, sugar and dairy produce, was established, and not by mass communications but by distribution networks that brought goods to the doorstep of the working population. Coming as it did soon after the Industrial Revolution, which had laid the foundations for a successful marketing nation, a growing and prosperous middle class, the marketing of the necessities of life achieved an unheard-of velocity.

The non-food producers soon recognised the advantages of establishing their own outlets where quality was assured and a successful sale earned a bonus, goodwill, towards a subsequent sale (a satisfied customer becomes a regular customer). And so the big names of today founded their businesses. Some, such as Boots, had been established earlier as pharmaceutical preparation manufacturers. They now wished to sell direct to the public by opening their own branches. Others, such as Marks & Spencer, began as retailers and extended activities into manufacturing later.

Even today mass marketing depends on effective distribution. No amount of advertising can force a sale if the product is not available at the customers' favourite outlet. Furthermore, a good advertising campaign may benefit competitors more than it does the advertiser if their distribution is better. Once interested in the idea of a particular product a consumer will soon try another offered by the retailer if the advertised product is not immediately available.

Nevertheless, mass distribution is difficult to achieve today without the support of an extensive promotional campaign. Retailers are faced with so many alternatives that they must discriminate in favour of those that will sell well and advertising, particularly on television, helps to achieve that objective. So selling to retailers must be accompanied by the promise of extensive promotional support.

Advertising as we know it today became possible following the advancement of communications. Yet it was dependent on the branding of goods. At one time the grocer stored products in jars or in sacks on the floor. As manufacturers became conscious of the need to provide guarantees of quality standards for their produce, they included their names on the goods. They also tried to make them as attractive as possible to consumers. So branding was introduced and the packaging industry received a stimulus which it believes, even now, is only the start of something big.

But today, even with branding and advertising established, it is still distribution that provides the way to successful consumer goods marketing. Advertising may make distribution channels more effective, but it cannot replace them entirely. Self-service and supermarkets are the major innovation in recent years, followed by mail order and direct response marketing providing further distribution channels. Even so, this twentieth-century revolution in distribution is considered the tip of the iceberg. For future generations, distribution must continue to be the significant element in the marketing mix, with consumer convenience being the major criterion for success, rather than price or even absolute quality standards. So finding the 'convenience' consumers need is the major marketing problem in consumer goods.

Industrial goods marketing

The Americans are often given the credit for establishing marketing practices. This is probably true of consumer goods, largely because the sheer vastness of the country provided the initiating distribution problem, but it is far from true as regards industrial goods. Industrial goods sales rely largely on the use of selling ability, a practical necessity that has been successfully employed by firms in the capital goods industries for longer than advertising has existed. Companies marketing industrial goods have had to create markets where markets did not exist before. Selling a tin of beans requires an identifiable purchaser who pays and reaps benefits. Building a bridge, a dam or a railway line, or installing a telephone network all provide very real benefits, to the entire population of a nation. Yet who pays? So when selling to governments, all of whom have to decide between bread today and jam tomorrow, it is essential to develop infrastructure and so ensure growth in market potential. In this way the capital goods industry is self-perpetuating, yet it must still feed off that growth.

Because of its overseas territories the UK had what amounted to captive markets. Moreover, because these territories needed industrial products in order to advance their own economies, they provided substantial growth and growth potential to the UK. But the country had to solve the problems of physical distribution first. The ox and the horse had been the major means of transport for many centuries, but they were inadequate for widespread and rapid distribution of capital goods. So railway networks, waterways and canals, shipping and port facilities became essential for industrialisation. British-owned, they provided the service factor essential to successful marketing. These investments provided the basis for the wealth of the British nation, and thus British industrial marketing led the world. However, these investments also laid the foundation for the present lack of growth of the country. The British people had too many vested interests to protect and, because of the extent of these interests, departures from traditional use tended to be avoided. Yet in this changing world expediency has become the critical factor in marketing. The British attitude of making one piece of equipment last longer than a lifetime became redundant. Now the life cycle of production machines has become significant. Reliability and long life are not as important as high production rates, flexibility to meet changing market needs, and equipment made at a price designed to bring a shorter life and rapid depreciation. Clearly economies of scale are better realised in new machines, operating at faster rates than would twice as many machines at slower rates. No better example is available than that provided by the British machine tool industry. It once led the world but is now being forced out of its own backyard by Japanese, German and American equipment. So to sell equipment the capital goods industry must sell ideas, and overcoming apathy is its major marketing task. For it must be remembered that all trading depends on consumer consumption. The ultimate aim of all manufacture, whether for the production of consumer goods or the assembly of capital goods

needed to produce consumer goods, is to satisfy consumer demand – the source of all monies and purchasing power.

The marketing of professional services

It is perhaps a paradox of modern life that the very area in which
marketing has been practised the longest is the one that has
acquired a reputation for lack of awareness in modern marketing
techniques. It is perhaps because the practice of marketing has so
long been a feature of the scene that it is now fully integrated and
not easy to identify, or even isolate. That is not to say that all
professional services are long established, for clearly many are the
result of scientific advances in this century. Hence the need for
specialisation – a division of labour in the intellectual sense. It is
true, however, that professional services do include the oldest
known to man. Unfortunately, in a discussion of the origins of man's
activities, good or bad, there is always some sensitivity – perhaps
because so many things that are sacred today grew from such
dubious beginnings that society does not wish to be reminded of
those earlier times. Even so, some practices are frowned upon
today, just as they were thousands of years ago. The pursuits
'health, wealth and stealth' are immortal. But we cannot ignore
history. The services of the witch-doctor, the alchemist, the prosti-
tute and the money-lender are but the origins of medicine, physics,
the theatre and banking. Politics grew out of oppression and
slavery, while early religion was based on fear of the unknown and
idolatry. But the unique characteristic associated with these early
services remains today. They all depend on faith – the psychological acceptance of some future satisfaction – for all provide post-
operative effects. This means that marketing evidence must be
based on credibility. Decisions as to the use of the service must be
made on personal judgment backed by knowledge and experience.
And once the service has been used there is no alternative against
which it can be measured. For the alternative, not using the service,
is liquidated the moment the service is put into operation. In this
sense measurement of the value of the service is indeterminate
except at an empirical level. Often it becomes pre-service hope
followed by post-service justification.

At the time of hiring a professional service the business executive cannot be sure of what he has bought. He feels the expectation that his problem may be overcome. But even then he cannot be sure that what he thinks his problem is will agree with that diagnosed by the professional.

So it will have to depend on trust, and that trust will only be formed when the professional has shown himself capable of under-standing the real problems of the client. Winning his confidence is therefore an essential ingredient.

It was suggested earlier that the marketing of professional ser-vices had a low profile because the practice of marketing had been fully absorbed into the service provided, mainly in the form of mystique, and so was indistinguishable from the actual facilities offered. This is, of course, a simplification, for many professional services reject, through their elected representatives, all forms of advertising and promotion as being unethical. In the UK the Monopolies Commission rejected the claims made by the profes-sions and implied that they were restrictive practices and not in the public interest. Clearly there is considerable scope for the enterpris-ing. But even so, the practitioner still has an opportunity to further marketing practice without offending his sincere, if out-dated, beliefs. Clean and attractive premises, modern equipment, warmth and comfort, civility from staff, and attention to the true interests of clients could benefit many. Belief in austerity, traditional methods, poor administration and complete disregard for any form of organ-isation is not the best recipe for overcoming the credibility gap – the marketing problem of the professions.

Nationalised industries

In attempting to retain community control over certain essential industries, society loses the benefits that competition forces on such organisations. Although some marketing techniques are employed by the Post Office and British Rail, for example, the normal limiting factors have not been present and the true services necessary for economic survival have evaporated. In establishing monopolies the pressure from market forces – the customer – has been weakened, and the power of the trade unions has been strengthened. At the same time the nationalised industries have become vehicles of government policy. Instead of consumer-dictated economic pressure, the conflicts have been between government and trade unions. However, privatisation may improve service, charges and facilities.

Marketing internationally

Marketing at an international level in any sophisticated sense is the baby of the marketing family. So far the youngster has used ideas borrowed from its brothers. Its own development seems to be dependent on the final rejection of the now long-established theory of comparative advantages. This theory suggests that a nation should concentrate its efforts on those goods and services that command a high return in export markets and import those that it cannot produce itself or for which it cannot compete on production costs. The disadvantage of this theory is that it assumes a more or less equal distribution of 'wealth' and a continuing demand for each type of goods and services compatible with the needs and aspirations, at any one time, of the nations so endowed. No one has yet resolved this problem. It has, moreover, been aggravated by the multi-national companies. Because of the sheer weight of resources put into an investment and because of the degree of automation achievable in modern manufacture, it is possible to site a new project in its most unlikely location and still produce goods at a cost advantage compared with older plants located in desirable spots and where vested interests exist. Recent investments in Eastern European countries and in the underdeveloped or developing regions are prime examples.

The answer to the problem may be global marketing, each nation behaving as a firm does, with a wide but comprehensive product range and a product mix subject to constant change. As each company within the nation of companies must seek top management approval for development plans and the receipt of capital funds, it must first justify its aims on a global scale. Of course, this happens now through the functioning of the money market. But this system is purely nationalistic, when what is needed is a global attitude. In fact, one must apply marketing principles to the trading problems of nations rather than just of companies. The employment of trading blocs is a step in the right direction, although these partnerships tend to be defensive rather than offensive.

The major drawback of such a solution is in the selection of top management. Yet there is a possible remedy. As the twentieth century has shown a redistribution of influence as well as of income and wealth, it should not be impossible for top management to consist of industrialists, academics, trade unionists and professional administrators seconded from their respective posts for a period. As educational standards improve, the disparity in knowledge should decline, even if historical ideas and beliefs tend to consolidate.

The major marketing problem remains. It is in the need for common acceptance of popular products – the 'standardisation' of cultural beliefs, social habits, and moral and religious behaviour.

Mini-marketing

Some planners believe that by the year 2000 industry and commerce will be in the hands of a mere 200 companies, basing their conclusions partly on current trends and partly on a belief in the economies of scale. These business prophets appear to have ignored the invaluable part played by small companies in forcing large organisations to realise the economies of scale. Without pressure from the small firm, big business has little incentive to utilise its capacity for improving efficiency.

Also ignored are the *competitive advantages* the smaller unit has over the bigger concern. A small firm with ambitions to grow is often better placed to take advantage of marketing opportunities than bigger companies. In an era of marketing consciousness, where the customer plays such a significant role in influencing commercial decision-making, it is the business that discovers and satisfies a need which prospers. The small company, because it has limited opportunities to use mass media and because the number of its customers is relatively low, is able to maintain a better line of communication with its markets at a personal level, through the salesman. Thus, like the early bird, it is able to see opportunities earlier. And because it does not have the cumbersome and complicated, yet essential, decision-making process of the larger organisation, it is able to initiate the means by which market innovation takes place. Equally, because buyers recognise the need for standardisation in the product range of big companies, they will take their special needs to the smaller firm. The result may be the springboard for a new product idea or, more simply, a 'special' for which the customer is prepared to pay a premium price.

Often a small business with low overheads, specialist skills, a limited product range, negligible marketing costs and established outlets with continual purchasing patterns (often found in the engineering industry) will be able to produce parts, subassemblies or components at a lower unit cost than a larger company. Similarly, in some industries there are few sales outlets and a limited demand for capital goods, which themselves are essential production units for large runs. The small firm is often the only unit inclined to develop an economic source of supply. Many buyers operating on behalf of international or multi-national companies favour the small firm to supplement the limited range of a major supplier and so help to ensure opportunity of choice as well as providing a lever to force improvements in service by the often indifferent larger organisation. Apart from helping to minimise the consequences of the growing monopoly being created by large multi-product groups, the small firm enables the economic system to run smoothly.

The small firm is the natural outlet for the energetic and determined individual who, perhaps having missed a satisfactory early education, decries the mediocrity of big business and its stifling effects on individual effort and enterprise. It is the ideal solution for enterprising and independent individuals whose vitality would be unsuited to the limitations of junior management in a large concern. It is this person, George Bernard Shaw's 'unreasonable man', whose entrepreneurial talent provides the initiative for devising and developing new products, techniques and services, a breeding ground for new industries.

The Report of the Committee of Enquiry on Small Firms (*The Bolton Report*) states: 'Apart from transport and communications, there are other aspects of marketing which have now come to enjoy substantial economies of scale. For example, improved techniques of distribution and the use of national media for advertising (themselves affected by technological change) are powerful factors working against the small firm. Indeed, we consider that lack of access (for the small firm) to economies in large scale marketing may be the most important single reason why the competitive strength of the larger firm has improved over the last fifty years.'

The small firms that are now forming marketing partnerships

believe that these will enable them to compete on equal terms in the areas of marketing practice so far dominated by big firms. In this way the small firm retains its independence while improving its long-term competitiveness.

The major problems of mini-marketing are in finding and exploiting minority needs. It has therefore a 'communication' problem to overcome. It must maintain contact with the few in the interests of the many.

Social marketing

Social marketing is now present on a large scale. While many believe it will have the greatest future growth rate of marketing expenditure, due to increasing social problems, it still has to secure the necessary funding. Spending tax-payers' money to, say, dissuade potential criminals, or to deter people from the hazards of smoking or drink-driving, does not meet with universal approval, while spending money to advertise the rights people may have to social benefits is not always viewed as an appropriate and necessary expenditure of money available.

Such attitudes may change, particularly if the expenditure is seen as being in some way self-liquidating, or is less expensive than traditional methods of communication and a cost-effective approach to social issues and problems.

The reader could not be blamed if, on reading this text, he is convinced that marketing is based on nothing more than common sense and the ability to communicate. He would be right. Unfortunately, common sense is rare, despite its name, and the ability to communicate equally rare. In combination their appearance represents a modern phenomenon. Finding personnel with the right talent is marketing's major continuing problem.

3

Marketing Research

The prime responsibility of the manager is decision-making. A decision is a conclusion or a formal judgment precipitating action. It is a process of evaluation and comparison. In order to evaluate and compare it is necessary to have information. Without information the basis for decisions is guesswork. Occasionally, due to the law of averages, such intuitive efforts succeed. Frequently, management actions are based on experience alone and some measure of success may be achieved for the same reason as intuitive actions.

Most managers will be aware of examples of successful ventures based on such meagre reasoning. With few exceptions, such successes will have resulted despite the lack of information, not because the information was unnecessary. Risk in business is endemic, but it should never be a gamble. In *The Verger* Somerset Maugham brought elementary market research graphically into perspective. The main character decided to open a tobacconist's shop after walking a considerable distance to make a purchase. As he explained, he knew from personal observation that the local demand was high. That decision was based on information, obtained at negligible expense; but even today projects costing many thousands of pounds are initiated without adequate consideration of supply and demand.

Marketing research is a process of investigation into the workings of the distributive systems. Henry Ford, as has already been mentioned, found through marketing research the price at which cars would sell by the million and then developed his mass production

techniques accordingly (see his autobiography, *My Life and Work*).
He was equating supply with demand.

Today, with the average size of company increasing, decisions
have become even more critical. While a bad decision involving
£20 000 by a small firm may have more disastrous consequences
than an equally bad decision involving £1 million or more by a large
firm, the bigger investment decision may take two years to implement and a further three years before the outlay is recovered
from profits. A time span of five years following a wrong decision
could mean lost opportunities, frustrated management and an
overall decline in company prosperity, far in excess of the project
costs.

Judged against the changes in the past five years – in product
innovation, channels of distribution, price levels and market
needs – decisions made today require knowledge of future environment, events and human behaviour. Research into these influencing
factors is essential.

It is almost 2500 years since Confucius said: 'Study the past if you
would divine the future.' At that time, communications, transport
facilities and human knowledge were decidedly poor. Production
was confined to single items, so remedial decisions were easily made
and quickly implemented. In the twentieth century this is not so.
Divining the future must be more sophisticated. Industry and
commerce is a mass of interdependent parts, cohesively manipu-
lated by governments, with its appetite both nourished and deprived by world trade and by technological progress. Thus the past
must be analysed, trends established and predictions made of
innumerable influencing factors. Marketing research will not determine the future, but it can be used to illuminate the scene, to
eliminate the unlikely and to spotlight the probable. It can help to
reduce business risk.

Investigating investment

Research need not be costly. It should cost neither less than is
justified nor more than is necessary in relation to the size or scale of
investment. For example, when buying a new hat it is usually
sufficient to visit the various stockists, compare styles and prices,
and, if satisfied, make a purchase. When purchasing a house, it is

normal for a more thorough investigation to be made. A survey of the property and its amenities is commissioned, and solicitors investigate legal title and any local planning developments. The prospective buyer, with the help of an estate agent, looks at local amenities, schools and recreational facilities. The building society will carry out its own independent inquiries. So the effort is equated according to the amount of expenditure. In each instance the extent of investigation is sufficient to meet the needs of the purchaser.

Many business decisions are made that could have been supported, or perhaps invalidated, by obtaining published information. Apart from internal records, most executives should be conversant with such official publications as *The Annual Abstract of Statistics*, *The Blue Book of Income and Expenditure*, the *Department of Employment Gazette* and the *Censuses of Distribution*. In addition to the wealth of Government publications, such bodies as trade associations, banks, chambers of commerce, embassies, national and local newspapers, and the trade and technical press publish reports that can be invaluable to commercial concerns. Many public libraries contain admirable works of reference and will often obtain information from other branches if it is not available locally.

One of the most comprehensive services provided for industry by the Department of Trade is the Statistics and Market Intelligence Library. Freely available for public use is a collection of trade and other economic statistics, trade directories and catalogues of manufacturers, which can be consulted either by personal visit, by telephone or by telex. Although the main purpose of the library is to provide a service in the field of foreign economic statistics, the library also holds complete sets of all the principal series of UK economic statistics.

An integral part of the British Institute of Management is the library at Management House. It contains the largest collection of management literature in Europe and includes much unpublished material not generally available in the UK. The library receives periodicals from all over the world; each is selectively scanned and indexed. Besides its lending services, the library has a valuable collection of reference material on management subjects. A wide range of specially prepared bibliographies helps those interested in particular subjects to keep abreast of current literature.

Apart from these libraries, there are many other sources of valuable information. The various National Economic Development Council departments prepare reports and publish their findings. Some trade associations make statistics available. *The Companies' Register* holds full financial information on all British companies, and many national newspapers maintain excellent information bureaux. *The Kompass Register* includes much company information and comprehensive details of products and services. There is a UK and an international edition of *Who Owns Whom*, compiled and published by Roskill & Co. *The Stock Exchange Year Book* is another valuable source of financial information.

Dun & Bradstreet publish a *British Middle Market Directory*, and *The Times* publishes annually a guide to the top 1000 companies in the UK. It is a visual comparative guide, by size and performance, to leading companies in the UK, the US, Europe, Japan and other countries. The top 1000 companies in the UK are ranked according to turnover and total sales. There is usually information on the fifty biggest mergers of the previous fiscal year. Apart from these sources there is a comprehensive list published by the Government Statistical Service, *A Brief Guide to Sources*, and the British Overseas Trade Board publish an *Export Services Handbook* which includes much valuable information and sources.

This list is not exhaustive and gives only an indication of the vast wealth of information readily available to industry. Few companies would fail to find some benefit in investigating sources relevant to their own operations.

Random sampling

Marketing research is frequently confused with market research. Marketing research is an activity that examines all the elements in marketing practice, including markets, products, distribution channels, pricing, consumer behaviour and opinions. Market research is but an element of marketing research, though easily the most widely known and practised. Opinion research is also a well-established operation. It has achieved recognition through public opinion polls. Predictions are made using sampling techniques, a fundamental part of marketing research. The concept of sampling (the law of probabilities) is that a number of items, if selected at random from a larger number of items, will tend to have much the same character-istics as the whole. Random selection means that every item of the whole must have a full and equal opportunity of being chosen.

In sampling a population of well over fifty million, complete 'random' selection is almost impossible to achieve. Opinion polls may be conducted in the streets and only persons accessible during that time are questioned. Where contact is made in the home, bias is possible as absentees are excluded and some people will not be willing to be interviewed; many others live in inaccessible places. Movement in population may be as high as 10% and so complete up-to-date lists will not be available.

In addition, whenever a mass selection of the population is sampled, there will be a certain error in the results, irrespective of whether the aim is to discover opinions of a political or commercial nature. Sometimes error can be introduced by smoothing or averag-ing. Since the adoption of a new code of practice for opinion polls, the five main companies in the field have been obliged to make available details of their methods of operation and the composition of their samples. The possibility of scrutiny should ensure that minimum acceptable standards will prevail. Nonetheless, such re-search activities are invaluable for policy or strategic decision-making. A 100% sample is almost impossible and would be un-realistic anyway; for example, only 70% or 80% of the population trouble to vote. Certainly in common research the limitations of sampling errors are more acceptable. Marketing executives are likely to understand the principles and will use the findings to exercise judgment and take action. They are another aid to deci-sion-making but should not be allowed to rule the decisions.

It is now comparatively rare for completely random samples to be prepared – quota sampling is more often used. This is a technique whereby a controlled sample is selected which is known to represent the characteristics of the whole. It is relatively simple to build up a sample based on occupational groups, geographical areas, age brackets and community size. Because the margin of error is measurable, it is possible to apply confidence factors to most survey results. The ratio of the sample to the whole is not significant. Whatever the number of items in the whole, a sample of between 200 and 3000 items would tend to reflect the characteristics of the whole. Certainly the greater the size of the sample, the greater the accuracy, but the additional accuracy rarely justifies the extra expense. After all, the sole purpose of marketing research is to improve profitability.

The researcher's role

The difference between consumer research and industrial research is in the techniques used. The number of potential customers in consumer goods usually outnumber those in the industrial field by multiples of thousands. Industrial outlets are sparsely spread and contact is often difficult and uneconomic. The industrialist may have a maximum of 300 outlets, of which perhaps twenty or thirty may consume the bulk of his output. He must therefore maintain contact with his customers, whatever channels of distribution he uses. If he uses distributors or agents he must ensure that the technical needs of his customers are satisfied. Because he must be in contact constantly and because the number of his potential outlets is limited, he is more easily able to obtain information. Similar market information could only come to the consumer-goods company through expensive field research. Usually the researcher in industry is expected to have related technical knowledge and relevant industrial background. In this way he will be able to win the confidence of both customer and employer, ensuring satisfactory communication between the two.

Field research may be conducted by postal questionnaire, telephone interviews or personal visits. Postal questionnaires have the advantage of economy, although the response rate may be low. Any conclusions drawn will have a built-in bias since people who tend to be mobile will not be represented, nor will those who habitually ignore research efforts. Telephone interviewing has the major advantage of time as contact is immediate and interviewers are able to explain the purpose of the survey. Answers may be recorded without the respondent being disturbed about the possible repercussions of his observations. The response rate is usually higher than with postal questionnaires. Bias is introduced because only those respondents available by telephone can be contacted. It is also impossible for the interviewer to obtain information by observation. Personal interviewing is usually the most reliable means of obtaining information, but it is expensive. To obtain the best results and to minimise the disadvantages of each technique, it is usual for a survey to use all three means of contact, structuring the sample according to predetermined criteria.

Questionnaire design

Most research studies are undertaken using a questionnaire. Often it is designed using principles established by a working study committee of the Market Research Society. As the research is carried out to determine a given business situation and the reasons for the currency of that situation, questionnaires are designed to help to assess the habits and prejudices of the chosen group of people that constitute the market. Clearly, to be useful and valuable, the answers must come as a result of well-worded and presented questions. To get the right answers one must ask the right questions. So a specific set of objectives is essential.

Questionnaires are used to ensure that the many interviewers being employed in different parts of the country carry out their interviews in as near identical fashion as possible. They ask the same questions and use the same terms. By using a questionnaire it is possible to ensure that answers provided by respondents, whether at a personal interview or otherwise, are recorded in a predetermined fashion. This makes it easy for the forms, and the answers, to be coded for analysis, particularly where a computer is to be used.

However, questionnaires have to be carefully designed. A poorly designed questionnaire will throw all the research findings into doubt, so its design must follow fairly simple principles. Providing the research project with a clear aim based on predetermined objectives is the first step. This should then be followed by a number of rules:

1　The central theme of the enquiry must be clear.
2　The interviewees' memories must not be overtaxed.
3　Every question must be clear.
4　Psychological factors must be anticipated.
5　Leading questions must be avoided.
6　Questions should follow a logical sequence.
7　The language of the informant must be used.
8　Questions must not restrict the interviewee.

9   Misleading questions must be avoided.
10   Questionnaires should be short and simple.
11   Questions should be confined to the personal experience of respondents.
12   Control questions should be introduced.

Although these rules may appear straightforward they are nonetheless broken sufficiently often to warrant an explanation.

1   The central theme of the enquiry must be clear
Enquiries are usually directed at particular users of a product, service or machine, so users must be identified in the first instance. If usage of the item concerned is the central theme of the research, then answers from non-users are irrelevant.

2   The interviewees' memories must not be overtaxed
People do not like to admit that their memories have failed them, particularly if there is an inference, as in a questionnaire, that they should be able to recall an event or incident. To overtax the interviewees' memories will introduce answers of doubtful validity and value.

3   Every question must be clear
Good communication is difficult to achieve and without supporting explanation often impossible. Yet to produce reliable information, unambiguous questions must be asked. So all questions need to be pre-tested. Studying the answers will indicate the clarity or otherwise of the questions concerned.

4   Psychological factors must be anticipated
Informants tend to offer what they consider to be the right answer rather than to express the exact truth. To a number of people an affirmative answer on usage of a deodorant could be taken as an admission of body odour. Similarly, the readership of quality newspapers is often overstated, as respondents give what are thought to be socially acceptable replies.

5   Leading questions must be avoided
People do not like to offend. In addition, experience has probably

taught them that contrary answers invite exploration and their time is limited. So they seek from tone, manner, gesture or whatever some sign of the approved or right answer. Any question that suggests a particular reply will most often get it. The results will therefore be invalid.

6   Questions should follow a logical sequence
As people are taught from the beginning of their education to think in sequence, it is advisable to follow that pattern. Most respondents will follow the sense of questions and so answers will come from reasoning rather than intuitively.

7   The language of the informant must be used
Many people use a language common to particular groups but foreign to outsiders. Accountants, engineers and, apparently, marketing men use their own special language – a practice to be avoided when questioning people who may not be aware of the special meanings that certain words have acquired.

8   Questions must not restrict the interviewee
The interviewee should be given a choice of possible answers to a question sufficient to produce the response most appropriate to his or her particular experience. To give straight alternatives makes choice difficult and sometimes onerous to people with knowledge lying somewhere between the extremes.

9   Misleading questions must be avoided
Misleading questions tend to arise whenever salesmen are used for research projects. It is not that they intend to mislead but that their enthusiasm is frustrated if the respondent ponders too long. So the salesman will try to help him out by asking a supplementary question which is often misleading.

10   Questionnaires should be short and simple
There is a common belief among market researchers that every question over twenty in number in a research study will cost 5% in lost response. Trying to extract too much information from one survey may therefore destroy the representative nature of the sample frame.

11 Questions should be confined to the personal experience of respondents

No matter how qualified they may feel to answer questions on behalf of their boss or spouse, third-party evidence is often totally misleading. It is difficult enough for the individual to know why a particular action is taken, let alone why someone else might do so. It is better for the researcher not to take the chance.

12 Control questions should be introduced

It is advisable to include a question that relates to an earlier one so as to establish a reliability factor in the informant. Sometimes researchers will also include a sample reliability question in order to test the validity of the selected sample.

These are sound principles of questionnaire design. Even when followed exactly it is still necessary to check whether the design is satisfactory. This is best done with a pilot test using about 10% of the proposed sample frame. A questionnaire should always be tested.

Depth interviewing

This is a technique used to discover the extent of a person's knowledge in a particular field and the underlying reasons behind his or her actions. It is not normally conducted using a questionnaire and tends to be much less formal, with the investigator guiding the conversation along from a list of points. The role of the interviewer is more like that of a prompter, even perhaps a sympathetic listener, rather than an examiner. The informant is allowed to develop his own lines of thought provided that they remain relevant to the enquiry. The major task of the interrogator is to help the respondent relax so that he is able to bring latent thoughts and motives to the surface.

It is generally believed that depth interviewing makes it easier to secure evidence of a person's attitude of mind or even his emotional feelings than is possible within the confines of a formal question-naire. Its greatest use perhaps is in the absence of other information, when material obtained using depth interviews may then be used in the construction of a questionnaire appropriate for a more formal study. Its enthusiasts claim that it is the only reliable means of testing advertising and sales promotional material. Presumably qualitative techniques of research into areas where publicity strategies are unavoidably qualitative has some logic. In practice there are good reasons why the technique has limited acceptance. Few people are capable of explaining their opinions and even fewer their emotions. So this makes the technique as vulnerable as formal questionnaires. Psychologists question the basis of the system, believing that the use of introspection provides a stimulus, for by the introduction of one thought we create another which was not present in connection with the held opinions. So a response would tend to be too educated to reflect the original view. In any case, usable conclusions cannot be expressed qualitatively and this makes it difficult to get some measure of the collective results.

It seems unlikely that depth interviewing will produce the results expected of it until some better means of interview recording is used, a realistic sample of consumers is tested so that standards of behaviour may be prepared and tabulated, and until psychologists are prepared to conduct the interviews rather than leaving them to unqualified researchers.

Behavioural research

Depth interviewing is now used to discover behavioural traits, attitudes, emotions, prejudices, norms, anxieties, and drives. These are the motives behind many purchasing decisions. People will go a long way and pay a lot to secure a little status, a little reassurance, or the prospect of a little romance. When they buy, they buy a dream, and they buy compulsively and impulsively, and will rationalise every decision with logical argument. Depth interviewing discovers those hidden motives, and will reveal the themes appropriate to advertising campaigns and the unique qualities applicable to brand properties.

Classifying the consumer

An analysis of research information would almost certainly prove fruitless if the total population were treated as one whole group. Clearly within one nation there are many subgroups that have characteristics common to the group and yet foreign to the remainder. The total population is therefore often divided into identifiable groups. These groups are normally:

1 Socioeconomic groupings
2 Sex
3 Age
4 Occupation
5 Area or region
6 ACORN – housing type location (see p. 183)

Apart from socioeconomic groupings, these classifications need no further explanation. Socioeconomic groupings leave much to be desired and are not now in general use. But they are still the subject of frequent reference in conversation, particularly in the advertising world. A means of categorising the nation is a vital aid to the mass media, particularly from a readership angle. However, there is no alternative to the socioeconomic group analysis. In this method the total population is subdivided by a combination of social position and earning power. For example, a member of the professional services, such as a barrister or a priest, will be included in the most affluent group irrespective of their earnings, qualifying because of their social position. Newspapers often provide information on their readership by socioeconomic groups. It enables them to help advertisers to decide the most appropriate medium for their campaigns. Clearly the more expensive commodities of life will be bought by the well-to-do and an advertisement aimed at them will appear in a publication popular in that group.

Consumer panels

Since the major benefit of market research is the discovery of trends and changes in purchasing habits, it is necessary to carry out research on a continuous basis rather than from time to time in an ad hoc fashion. These continuous research studies enable advertisers to observe consumers' changing tastes, their buying habits, opinions and brand preferences. So declines in sales can be anticipated and remedial action taken. The sample used in these studies is semi-permanent and questioning is undertaken at regular intervals. These samples are known as panels and may be either groups of dealers or groups of consumers. The dealer panels provide a valuable insight into the attitudes of the trade towards a company and its products. The consumer panels, however, provide the most critical information and have many positive benefits:

1 Trends can be established.
2 Past behaviour is already recorded.
3 The cost of the panel may be shared.
4 The nature of the research allows intimate questioning.
5 It is not necessary to rely on consumers' memories.
6 Unreliable informants are soon spotted and dropped.
7 Changes in tastes precipitate action in the market place.

A number of disadvantages, however, are apparent. Maintaining the panel and its members' cooperation is a continuing problem, while having to submit to the discipline of a regular record of behaviour tends to inhibit natural behaviour. The administration of the panel can be expensive, requiring constant checking of detail and supervision of certain members' tendency to understate their purchases of cheaper brands.

Retailer audits

The Nielsen Continuous Index type of research was introduced into the UK just before the outbreak of the Second World War. It consists of a team of auditors who make regular visits to a selected panel of retailers representative of the retail trade and count the actual stock and invoiced purchases for the period since the last count. Its major benefit in research terms is as a measure of the flow of goods to consumers. As such, it provides information on the rate at which goods are passing through the channels of distribution.

When a product goes out of fashion its sales will decline at the point of purchase, but the trade may still order as before and there may be no indication of the forthcoming calamity. And, of course, the trade will not appreciate being left with unsaleable goods.

Nielsen's provide a fairly comprehensive coverage in their reports, but the following categories are typical:

1 Sales to consumers by product and by brand.
2 Sales to retailers by product and by brand.
3 Current stocks by product and by brand.
4 Percentage of outlets handling the various brands.
5 Percentage of outlets with stock outs for various brands.
6 Retail and wholesale selling prices by product.
7 Volume of business handled direct and through wholesalers.
8 The extent of display and the sales scheme in operation at each outlet by various brands.

This service enables the subscriber to vet trends among his own and his competitors' brands, and to isolate problem areas by one or more of the main geographical regions or by one or more of the three sizes of shop shown. It means that every manufacturer knows the share he has and the changes in shares between himself and his competitors. This information is more than just useful. It can indicate how a company's growth in sales compares with growth in the total market and, if there is a decline, whether it is confined to the company or is industry-wide. The indices provided by the Nielsen organisation cover food, drugs, tobacco, pharmaceuticals and confectionery. The firm also produces an index on liquor from Scotland.

Many of the benefits of the system approximate to those listed under consumer panels. In addition, it provides information on distribution of a product, effect of price changes, promotions and advertising. But it tends to be expensive, is not truly representative because some multiples will not cooperate, and figures are calculated in complicated forms, not always inspiring confidence in the heart of the subscriber. By definition its findings are quantitative, so although it indicates what, where and when it does not provide information on the vital areas of why and how.

Test marketing

The value of test marketing is hotly disputed. Its supporters believe it is the only means by which a company is able to overcome teething problems before going national and before irreparable damage takes place. Others say that it warns competition, and that regions do not truly reflect national characteristics and therefore tests are invalid.

Clearly there is sense in each argument. The organisers of test marketing operations must, therefore, recognise the limitations of the technique and use it to their advantage. The best value can be obtained in:

1 Formulating a national introductory plan.
2 Deciding the best media available for the product.
3 Choosing the most effective level of advertising.
4 Selecting the appropriate price level for maximising profit.

The golden rule is to carry out tests in at least two areas and to investigate every disparity that arises. In each area the tests should be considered as separate activities.

A test will fail if the new product is given special support while in the introductory stage. Even the presence of the marketing manager during the launch constitutes additional support. The most usual support of this sort discovered is:

1 Presence of 'authority' at local branch.
2 Heavier advertising support than is possible nationally.
3 Giving the product a 'fair chance' by using the best territory or the best salesman as a testing ground.

To be considered successful a product must stand the test of time – the time to include repeat purchases. Where national performance lags behind the hopes generated for it by the test market, it is either because of the overemphasis already described or because the decision to launch nationally has been taken before the test promotion has matured.

Conditions for concluding that the new product satisfies the test marketing objectives are:

1 That initial response has been generated according to plan.
2 That repeat purchases are now being made.
3 That the consumer is making repeat purchases in normal conditions and not in the tidal wave of launch.
4 That the longer term (six months to a year) shows a steady acceptance of the product and continuing growth.

5   When inconsistencies in plan appear and are resolved through contingencies.

It should be understood that test marketing is not a product test. The product will have been tested and tried prior to the pilot venture. The test marketing project is to test the *marketing* of the product – to confirm the adequacies of the planned marketing mix. However, it can often be used as a final test of *acceptance* for the product, although in a sense this is a check on the company's ability to market the product and not a trial of the product's worthiness.

Measuring advertising effectiveness

Some activities of marketing can be quantified in some way. One exception is advertising. To some companies the advertising appropriation is the biggest single item of expenditure in the marketing budget. Yet no one has been able to measure the extent to which advertising increases sales. Because advertising is usually so closely tied to exploiting the concept of marketing, it is not always possible to isolate it from other marketing activities. There are some exceptions. Mail order houses are able to measure trends in effectiveness because advertising and sales promotion is almost all of their promotional effort. We do, however, know that advertising works. We may not know the exact level at which expenditure may be justified, but we do know that the expenditure can be effective.

How, then, can one deal with advertising expenditure objectively? A change in attitude and approach is necessary. The businessman must move away from attempting to measure the effectiveness of the advertising *function*, which is to *inform* and to *persuade*. As the basis of marketing research is one of evaluation and comparison, a standard of performance must be established. Without a predetermined standard, objective measurement is not possible. The critical issue is: 'what do we want our advertising to achieve?' If it is necessary, for example, to increase public awareness of the product, then this will be the advertising objective. Research may reveal that only 10% of prospective customers know of a product. Research may show that the other 90% can be contacted through a given medium. The campaign, the appropriation and advertising objectives thus become clear. Measurement of effectiveness is made by further research to reveal the increased awareness of the product by the market.

Marketing research is a valuable tool of management. The growing complexity of business operations makes its greater and more widespread use essential. It is a vital part of profit planning and needs to be used to obtain information essential for decision-making.

4

Product Planning and Pricing

To understand marketing philosophy it is first necessary to consider the nature of product satisfaction. For what is a product? Consider jewellery. Does the average person buy an expensive ring because of the utility of this purchase or is there some underlying purpose? Why should a person 'trade-up' from a Mini to a Rover? For what reason do people buy cosmetics? A jewel may have no real value, while a Mini will take a person from one place to another quite satisfactorily, and cosmetics are but waxes and greases of comparatively little value in the untreated state. Clearly the purchaser is buying some satisfaction which is identified with the product rather than with the primary purpose for which the product has been made available.

A ring denotes genuine affection. It has connotations with love and marriage. Between young people it is, perhaps, the ultimate material gift. It signifies the value placed on the relationship and the durability of the union. It suggests promise for the future – a promise of happiness even – together. Similarly, buying a more expensive car is a symbol of progress. It is a gesture of defiance to friends, or a quest for approval from relations, and an expression of self-assurance before the opposite sex, for the motor car has been described as the ultimate sex symbol. And cosmetics are not required because of their ability to create beauty but because of their confidence-building capacity. It follows that the purchasers of these products are, in turn, buying a symbol of love, social approval and self-confidence. So the product concerned, for each of them, does no more than provide the means by which a need is fulfilled. Thus a product may be defined as a 'conveyor-belt of satisfactions', not so very different in meaning from the classical economists' 'bundle of utilities'. The important factors are that totally different products may be competing against each other for the same purpose, while marketing communications aimed at *product utility* will have little or no effect on consumer motivation.

In today's society output at one factory may have little to distinguish it from the output of a competitive factory. In the market place, however, the same products may have totally different sales performances. Because the marketing of one product may have provided so much 'added value' it becomes a much better proposition to the buyer. So the product must provide satisfaction to innate desires as well as function mechanically, and it must be marketed in a way that enables the buyer to achieve the greatest possible satisfaction at the lowest possible expenditure of time, effort and money. Products need to conform to this specification in order to succeed. But success is relative, for some successes are confined to a few short months, while others may endure for many generations.

Endowing a brand with an abstract association of ideas, a unique benefit aimed at emotional needs, gives a product a virtual monopoly, a haven from competition, and a franchise in the mind of the consumer. This is crucial to brand strategy in marketing. Product planning is based on segmentation, brand differentiation, and promotion through perceptive selection.

This principle is applied to product portfolio analysis. By reviewing brands in the product range for marketability the company attempts to develop a product mix that fully coordinated will produce an optimum balance between supplies, production, distribution, and marketing and therefore the ultimate in profitability. To do this the company expects to be able to manage demand by mass production of customers at the level and to the price it wishes. It can do this only by the segmentation principle, applied to each of its brands.

The product life cycle

Fashion goods may enjoy buoyant sales for one season only, while basic industries such as coal or iron extraction have experienced growth in sales performance for centuries. Yet in each case it is necessary for the marketing executive to recognise the evolutionary nature of each product's life span. The marketing executive associated with fashion goods knows that the market situation is volatile and that a constant stream of new designs is essential. For without new creations the fashion industry would cease to be in *fashion* and would have to resort to *clothing*. Fashion is a more attractive market because the level of expenditure necessary to accommodate a person's need for style is greater than their level of expenditure on clothes for warmth, modesty and convention.

In the extractive industries the position is quite different, for coal and iron ore remain much the same, despite frequent attempts to improve the product. But the marketing manager has an equally arduous task, because although he has little chance to adapt the product he has almost complete versatility in the market segments open to him.

In each case the product life cycle has similar characteristics but the time span is different. Moreover, that time span puts different pressures on the marketing team and the company's corporate strategy evolves accordingly. Each product goes through four stages: introduction, growth, maturity, decline.

The duration of each stage varies considerably. Clearly the use of the product life cycle concept is only of real value if each stage in its curve is predictable, because once achieved it would suggest a means by which demand could be varied according to the level of marketing expenditure, and so it would bring a revolution in marketing practice with enormous consequences.

1 Understanding the market

The share of a specific market obtained by any particular company is subject to constant change. It may be caused by pricing strategy, by product innovation or by new product development. The forces of competition are among the most difficult to predict of all the variables facing the businessman. It is not always easy to decide which competitors are most likely to be active at any foreseeable time in the future. It is necessary, however, to prophesy which products from the competitors' ranges, and which of their areas, are likely to be given special promotion.

Frequently the decisions made within a company will be the result of internal political manoeuvring and strength of personality. Even these influences are subject to rapid change. Often a particularly aggressive promotional campaign by one company will expand the total market and others will benefit. For example, when a manufacturer of soups with a 50% level of distribution among retail outlets advertises on television, he may stimulate interest and invite consumers to try the product for the first time. Those enquiring at their local store and finding the goods unavailable may be diverted to an alternative. The same principle can apply in industrial markets. A salesman may interest a prospect in a money-saving piece of equipment. The prospect may then contact his regular supplier of industrial equipment, with whom he has a good relationship, hoping he has a similar product. This stimulus may even produce a demand for suitable alternatives. The businessman who has been interested by a computer salesman may begin investigations in data processing in general and, for example, decide on a real-time computer service. Hence there would be little change or upheaval, so frequently associated with the installation of a computer, in his present system of working.

So, in evaluating competitive influences, it is necessary first to evaluate the impact general economic influences may have upon the industry as a whole. Frequently government legislation can cause a shift in the pattern of demand; for example, discontinuing tax concessions for entertainment expenditure caused a temporary setback to many catering establishments. Money not spent on entertainment was then channelled into other areas. Often the growth of a totally unrelated industry affects the performance of others. The rapid growth of the petro-chemical industry and the increasing use and storage of combustible materials have probably stimulated the demand for fire detection, alarm and defence systems, particularly sprinklers. Fortunately, many of these external influences are predictable. Certainly there will be any amount of published comment and opinion which will often indicate likely possibilities. Usually trade associations and professional institutions make representations on proposed government legislation, while recognised authoritative writers suggest the possible consequences of economic developments. For the vigilant, external influences to a particular industry can be noted and the consequences assessed. Constant review of the trade and technical press, the business news and city sections of national newspapers helps the enlightened businessman to ensure that he is aware of future events and possibilities.

Monitoring external influences becomes more complex during periods of economic instability. It may still be necessary to evaluate the extent to which competitors are likely to affect business prospects during any given period of time. Often competitors for available purchasing power become confused with competitors for substitute products. Sausage is easily recognisable as a substitute for meat but during hard times bread and potatoes – competitors for purchasing power – become substitute products as well: *less* meat, *more* potatoes. A competitor evaluation is an integral part of the marketing plan, for, whether active or passive, all competitors' actions influence the performance of other companies within the industry. If a company is experiencing a bad spell or liquidation, its death throes could cause an upheaval in the market. It may choose price cutting as the easiest solution to its problems; other companies anxious to maintain their market share may match the lower prices, and the general level of profitability will drop.

Apart from price cutting, the events that frequently cause a change in the usual market pattern are:

(*a*) Product innovation
(*b*) Product substitution
(*c*) Government legislation
(*d*) Product obsolescence
(*e*) Changes in taste or fashion
(*f*) Seasonal factors
(*g*) Import quotas
(*h*) Trade recessions
(*i*) Strikes and industrial disputes
(*j*) Changes in distribution margins

2   Investigating the competition

To decide just what course of action competitors are likely to take in any given circumstances will frequently be perplexing. Often information is obtainable with little effort. Customers often report a planned launch of a new product by a competitor. To obtain information on the likely sales strategy may be possible by watching the classified advertisement columns of the trade and technical press or of the national newspapers. It is surprising how much useful information companies reveal in their search for staff. Even the use of box numbers or selection consultants does not always conceal a company's identity, particularly to the discerning businessman who has anticipated some such action on the part of a competitor.

When no supporting information is available, the best action to take is to consider what information would be needed to make a decision and what choice would be made if the investigator had to decide. This rule of thumb usually produces a number of logical paths that may be taken, each of which may produce similar results. So, from an infinite number of variables, the choice has been reduced to just a few. Flexible counterplans may now be prepared which can be actioned as soon as further information becomes available. In a number of instances it is known that competing marketing executives exchange information relevant to their development.

The 1967 Companies Act made it possible for an investigator to obtain substantial financial information on competitors. The exempt private company no longer exists; such companies are compelled by law to file a profit and loss account and a balance sheet with their annual returns. Information about companies is readily available from Companies' House in London. However, a breakdown between product groups is not provided. So companies competing against others with diverse product ranges and selling to different markets will have some difficulty in assessing the sales turnover achieved by those companies in the field being investigated.

In making a comparison between competitive firms it is logical to assume that, whatever the extent of market penetration achieved by firms, the success or otherwise of their achievements is attributable to some activity on their part. One firm may have a strong sales force, another may spend considerable sums on advertising. Whatever the cause, it should be isolated. In drawing up a league table of competitors the businessman should develop a means of weighing up these activities. They will vary according to industry, but they will normally include:

(a) Pricing strategy
(b) Sales-force strength

(c)   Advertising effectiveness
(d)   Product advantages
(e)   Past reputation
(f)   Distribution facilities

By progressively developing a league table it should soon be possible to establish measurement of the comparative effectiveness of the tools of marketing activity. Combining these factors with changing market shares should indicate the division into which future promotional budgets should be prepared.

3   Attracting new product ideas

In this competitive environment unique product advantages are short-lived since others will copy successful innovation or make further improvements. If the growth rate of net profit is to be maintained a company must initiate a new product-development programme, particularly when confronted with escalating marketing costs for established products. Even those companies that have already established new product departments need to improve still more the ratio of successful to unsuccessful products. There are three different methods by which new product ideas can be brought to the attention of a company.

Members of the sales force constantly report on ideas given to them by customers and prospects, while the company's own production and research people and executives will be constantly suggesting new product possibilities. Outside the company, suggestions may come from independent inventors, distributors, suppliers, advertising agents, the trade press and even competitors.

The ideas emanating from external sources are usually spontaneous thoughts which may or may not have validity in terms of markets sales potential. Often external ideas are the major source of suggestions and the system frequently brings a high failure rate.

Less frequently, but more effectively, a company may make a conscious effort to study systematically the markets it satisfies in an endeavour to establish new needs, or old needs that have never been properly satisfied. This is known as *gap analysis*, and where opportunities are uncovered a suitable product can be introduced and the known benefits heavily promoted.

Resources

Logically, this approach could be adopted by all companies; it makes use of present market knowledge, is within the company's own business activity and in an area of operation where marketing skills have already been tried.

In evaluating such needs a company may find that a small company has been specialising in the satisfaction of a current need but does not have the resources, or perhaps the inclination, to develop the market to its full potential.

The acquisition of such a company may prove a sound investment, as established business can be obtained with much of the development costs written off, together with personnel having experience and knowledge of uses to which the products may be put and of the applications that have already been established.

The new product-development team must be assured of a constant stream of ideas from the sources already suggested or as a result of regular brain-storming sessions. Ideally, new product ideas will come from the marketing research team, although occasionally suggestions from research and development may need to be tested in terms of market acceptability before any attempt is made to commercialise them.

Before finalising a development programme it is always advisable to carry out a preliminary appraisal of the commercial feasibility of each project. This study should include desk research in an effort to compile as much associated information as possible relevant to the product's development, production, promotion and acceptance.

At the same time the researchers will have consultations with all known qualified opinion from within the company and, as far as possible, outside the company. Attempts will have to be made to test the likely market sales potential and the sales volume that may be achieved at each time-stage after the product's launch. The expected product design and specification is identified and recorded, while all packaging considerations are listed.

A network of timing for launch and related promotional activities is prepared with pricing proposals clearly shown, along with the anticipated costs of capital development. Additional labour requirements are specified and the promotional and other marketing costs budgeted.

Sales volume

If after this thorough screening process the new product idea is considered satisfactory, a full development programme may be formulated with confidence. In making this feasibility study the company is clearly basing its future upon perceived and measured market needs.

At the outset it should be established whether the new product is intended to bring a higher sales volume in order to take up surplus manufacturing capacity or whether it is intended to provide more profitable sales volume by replacing, ultimately, products that may have a declining rate of profitability.

Any such policy statement should specify whether an expansion, or more successful operation, is intended in established markets or whether an entry is planned into new markets which may offer better profit potential.

When entering a new market, executives tend to recognise the limitations of their market knowledge and even consider deeply the possible inadequacies of their marketing effort in promoting the new product successfully. What many executives do not recognise is that with a constantly changing market situation the same principle will often apply to the market with which they do have knowledge and experience.

Test marketing a product in a chosen area which statistically and by observation tends to represent the characteristics of the total market is used effectively by a number of companies. One of the most difficult parts of test marketing is, in fact, the selection of the trial area. It is never easy to choose the necessary level of expenditure for one isolated area that would equate with a national launch. An area is usually chosen because it contains sufficient purchasers to provide a realistic sample and yet is small enough to be covered economically with suitable control.

Purchasers

To market an industrial product, which may vary in sales volume according to the type of purchaser, it is necessary to establish the different types of purchasers in the test area and how they compare with the national concentration. The area must be one that has advertising media and a local sales force which are typical of the whole country.

If the new product is intended to fill a gap in an existing range, the competitive strength of the launching company must be compared with that of others in the area and related to national market shares before any worthwhile conclusions can be drawn.

4 Developing the product image

Even selling internationally, the marketing man must strive to create a product image. People tend to associate countries with certain goods and services. For example, Switzerland will be associated with banking services and winter sports; Holland with diamonds, tulips and cheese. Most industrially advanced countries can be associated in this way with particular products. In many instances the product and the country of origin have become linked together – Scotch whisky is the prime example. In overcoming such established images the marketing man may have to spend considerable time in educating his future market.

Many goods once considered luxuries are now accepted as necessities of life. Since the day when Henry Ford set out to find the price at which cars would sell by the million, manufacturers have increasingly tried to price their products to appeal to mass markets. Inevitably this has meant standardisation. Popular prices can be achieved only through mass production, and mass production must mean the elimination of some choice. The larger firms usually concentrate on satisfying the mass markets, with consumers clamouring for goods that they can now afford. Without large-scale production and the prices that result, most consumers would be unable to buy these goods. The limitation of choice is the additional price to be paid for such products. The smaller firm tends to concentrate on the provision of more specialised goods which the minority will always demand and for which they are prepared to pay a higher price.

In developing mass markets the larger manufacturer must devote his total resources to promoting popular products through emphasis on particular qualities that the product possesses. Sometimes these benefits may be apparent, but often they are contrived in order to provide a company with a unique selling proposition. In creating a unique image companies frequently achieve a monopoly. This monopoly is a direct result of brand loyalty and not because of limitation on sources of supply. Often the manufacturer's name becomes almost a generic term for the product itself. Few people would need an explanation of the products associated with Hoover, Scotch Tape or Biro. Occasionally, such manufacturers are able to charge a premium on the price of their products.

It is on perceptive interpretation of potential markets needs that progressive companies prosper. It is by finding a need, assessing the potential and, where substantial, taking the necessary action to satisfy the need that true market orientation becomes apparent. It is not enough for companies to provide production capacity. The market for a product has to be prepared, particularly where the need is still latent.

Pricing

It seems common among firms for pricing decisions to be made on the information supplied by accountants based on analysis of costs. Although most trained managers would recognise this as inadequate, few are able to suggest the means by which a better alternative, the market price, is implemented. For although market pricing may be the accepted technique, the experts are unable to produce the evidence upon which such a price may be calculated.

The market price itself escapes definitive expression. After all, many firms are unable to define their market, let alone the prices its members would be prepared to pay. Most suppliers are unable to put a 'cost' on the market value of a product acceptable to its purchasers. This is hardly surprising when one considers the disputed alternatives on return-on-investment appraisal. Probably the purchasing company itself does not know the value of a capital equipment purchase. If it does, it is unlikely to be adamant about the accuracy of its calculations, and it is certainly equally unlikely to reveal its costings to a supplier. A wholly-owned subsidiary may be prepared to release such calculations; in fact, it probably had to, to gain top management approval for the investment, so the figures would be available. But, judging by the controversy over transfer pricing, it seems unlikely that associated companies are in a position to help each other over the calculation of a market price. Moreover, the market price itself may not be at one level; it may even be possible at a number of platforms. The total potential demand for a product may therefore range between broad parameters. People buying a Rolls Royce motor car may be quite indifferent to the price. In fact, if the price were doubled, it is conceivable that the demand would grow because the value of certain goods is judged by price alone. Consider this example. An importer sold a small consignment of Russian salmon to a retailer. Some weeks later the importer checked and found that the retailer had sold one tin. On hearing that the one sale had been 'for the cat' and that it had been sold at 20p compared with the price of 80p for the regular English tin, he, the supplier, suggested a selling price of £1·60. As a result, the consignment was sold in three days. It had sold as a luxury product comparable even to caviar.

Greengrocers and fruiterers are well aware of the peculiarities of the consumer. Put a case of apples up for sale at 30p per lb and sales will be moderate. Put the same apples in three displays selling at 25p, 30p and 35p and sales will be healthy, particularly at 30p. When the display at 30p is emptying it is replenished from the other two. People like to choose something to suit their own individual ideas, and usually it will not be too dear and certainly not the cheapest. A certain butcher has a thriving business because he knows how to treat his customers. One late arrival seeing a solitary chicken in the display cabinet asked if he had anything larger. Taking the last bird with him into the walk-in ice-room he said he had been closing up for the day and that there were others in the store. Returning in seconds with the same bird and a higher price tag he enquired if this one would do. The customer was delighted. He charged her the original lower price and everyone was happy.

Incremental pricing theory

Pricing has such problems. A story originating from Roy Jenkins of Quantum Sciences Ltd is an example of profitable pricing 'under cost':

A barrow boy sets out from home in the morning with £75 in his pocket and buys fifty shirts. He sells his first one at 9.00 a.m. for £3 and thinks 'that's a start, we'll see how they go at that'. By midday he has sold twenty-five at £3 each. After lunch he sells another at £3 and thinks 'that's a £3 profit'. At 4.00 p.m. he has ten left and sells them at £1 each – still at a profit. The last one he sells to the man at the next barrow for 50p – still at a profit. Accountants will shudder.

These concepts of profit are very easy to apply in such circumstances, but they become so much more complex in larger organisations and where many people and activities are involved. Yet the basic principles still apply. Many an organisation will sell the bulk of its output below its computed 'cost', because the cost includes a full recovery of overheads at a particular level of operation. Change that level and the whole cost structure alters. But selling the bulk of its output below this cost enables the company to use production systems totally uneconomic at a smaller scale but highly cost-effective at the level at which the firm operates. The profitability achieved on the balance of its production overcompensates for the prices charged to the big buyers. The supplier is maximising his profits. This incremental costing system carries risks. But the profits it earns are the rewards it gets for risk bearing.

Pricing in the marketing mix
Because so many companies choose to use prices as their major strategy, pricing has been assured a position of isolation from the marketing mix. Moreover, because of this, it is essential to differentiate between pricing strategy and pricing tactics. This is not always easy because they are often interdependent. A company may decide to slot into a particular market at a specific price level and it develops a product accordingly. This is pricing strategy. It is the basis of Henry Ford's success with the Model T and is the underlying strategy behind the Japanese growth. The organisation aims at the most vulnerable price level ripe for exploitation. Once the price level has been established, necessary variations in the price structure day to day are tactical.

Price is, however, but one element in the marketing mix. Often it is no more than a substitute for other marketing activities. A low pricing level may be a substitute for a strong sales force, or it may be an alternative to promotional activity. Although it has been shown that sound marketing reduces prices, it is often pressure from the least efficient concerns, those that cut prices to survive in the face of powerful marketing, that brings the industry price level within the pockets of the less well-to-do.

Pricing techniques
Most companies are engaged in a marketing battle which is attempt-

ing to break the incidence of demand curves or at least to bend them in their own favour. The usual techniques for this objective are:

1 Penetration price
2 Skimming price
3 Competitive price
4 Diversionary price
5 Dumping price

1 Penetration price
This is the technique whereby the company enters the market at a price lower than that of the competition in order to win market share. It is mostly used in markets where there is little brand loyalty and customers are highly responsive to price moves. It is particularly advantageous when a new entrant develops a technological breakthrough, is able to offer output profitably at 10% below competition price, and so forces the less cost-effective companies out of the market. It is, however, a poor technique when used in markets with high brand loyalty or where considerable technological knowledge is applied, for it tends to compel reciprocal action and the net result is depressed prices with no one materially better off.

2 Skimming price
In the use of this technique the company concerned is endeavouring to up-market its product so as to improve further on quality, service and expenditure on marketing costs, and thus capitalise on its efforts. There is sufficient evidence to show that companies with high price tags ride the storms of depression more easily than cut-price merchants, mainly because the additional margin gives them more room to manoeuvre.

3 Competitive price
This is the common price around which most firms tend to bunch their quotes. It is frequently a cost-plus based estimate and tends to be used in fairly large stable markets. In such markets it is usually possible to make reasonably accurate sales estimates.

4 Diversionary price
The true price of products is not easily calculated because it is

hidden by additional charges for extra necessary services. An example may be wall-to-wall carpeting in the home or a turnkey operation in industry.

5 Dumping price
This is a process by which the supplying company offers products at a price 'below cost' but which, because of the marginal revenue/cost concepts, allows the company involved to make additional profits. The term usually refers to overseas trading, but is just as applicable in the home market. The principle is often practised where the manufacturer has one really large account buying below cost and, because of the volume handled, higher profits are made on the balance of the business than would have been possible if that business had had to stand alone.

It is sometimes, though not always, the practice adopted to supply major retail outlets with 'own-label' products.

Pricing for profit

While most firms strive to achieve a specific percentage return on output, they often fail to recognise that they are in effect standardising their opportunities. Although in discussion the managers concerned would agree that each product in the range requires a different investment in marketing costs, they nevertheless, in practice, allow all products to carry an equal absorption rate. This is a dissipation of effort. Some products supported by concentrated marketing effort could be sold at higher prices and at greater volume, while other products would not change in sales volume if no more than 1p were spent on promoting them. So while one product is ripe for exploitation and another already fully exploited, they still get an even amount of effort both in expenditure and in activity. This is a waste of company resources. And it is the major area where improved productivity in marketing is necessary and likely. Because it dictates the company's product mix policy, it is a key area for improvement in profitability. Although the pricing factor is a significant consideration, it is secondary to understanding the customer – a prerequisite of marketing orientation. It is the essence of product planning and pricing.

5

Marketing Planning

Marketing planning begins with the determination of marketing goals and develops through consideration of how these goals may be achieved. As a number of alternative courses will always be open to management, it is necessary for information to be obtained so as to aid problem-solving and ease decision-making. In this way planning is concerned with formalising management aspirations and with the quantity and the quality of effort needed to satisfy these ambitions. It is also involved with the company's ability to generate the necessary effort from all available resources.

Marketing planning shares with the other activities of the marketing mix the distinction in commerce of being a dynamic element in the business operation. Planning is dynamic because it provides a compulsive force; *it compels*:

1 The determination of real goals.
2 The exploration of different markets and the latent potential necessary to achieve real goals.
3 The systematic evaluation of the different product ideas needed in those markets.
4 A choice of marketing strategy appropriate to achieve anticipated market sales potential.
5 The consideration of the best type of organisation to exploit the situation.
6 The adoption of a monitoring system relevant to the chosen commercial operation.

This compulsive force indicates the real and lasting value of the modern planning process; the true benefits of planning come from the purely conceptual and mechanical effort needed to establish and maintain a plan. The thinking through of problems and the fullest consideration of the management consequences following the introduction of any of the different remedial measures available provide the basis for success. In planning, the rewards come from what is put into the plan rather than from what is eventually published.

The role of government in planning

Both government on the one hand and industry, trade and commerce on the other each have a leading role in forecasting and in the decision-making necessary for acceptable planning. In Europe there is disagreement about the benefits or otherwise of formal planning. The French are convinced planners and believe that governments should set growth rates and investment targets for each industry, together with a national economic growth rate. These plans are coordinated through committees of business, trade unions and government officials. The German view, however, is quite different. They say that the French are simply adding up opinions and that, no matter what sophistication is used, it is not possible to produce reliable figures by totalling personal views. They refuse to accept that a sum of qualitative statements makes a quantitative realistic target. But the Germans do accept the need for planning although arguing that forecasts should be considered no more than indicative.

In the UK the two leading political parties are credited with contrasting beliefs, one believing in a planned economy and the other in a free economy. The truth would show both parties somewhere between these parameters, with neither wishing to adopt, completely, an extreme doctrine. All British governments in recent years have set themselves clear policy objectives: the maintenance of employment, satisfactory balance of payments, reasonable price stability and a minimum economic growth. In essence they have taken as their first priority the task of controlling the overall level of demand in the economy. The second task of government has been to encourage the full play of competitive forces. The Monopolies Commission and the Restrictive Practices

Court are the vehicles for the implementation of parliamentary policies in this respect.

The nature and purpose of central planning
In the modern world most of the advanced nations have mixed economies, often with government spending in significant proportions. In order to obtain the funds necessary to carry out its programme every government must maintain taxation, with revenue coming from individuals and corporations alike. Moreover, as essential services are often provided by public corporations such as the Post Office, these provide each government with considerable economic power and influence. As the larger part of manufacturing industry and commerce is governed by economic market forces, it does not automatically follow that long-term, nor short-term for that matter, national needs are being met. So the government intervenes and encourages the redirection of industry and the redeployment of resources. Equally, the forces comprising the market economy do not always work quickly enough to avoid violent swings in demand, so the government tries to provide a stabilising force and to control fluctuations within desirable limits.

Because the nation enjoys the benefits accruing from economies of scale, investment decisions in new productive units, often involving substantial sums, need to be taken well in advance of actual demand. Because idle plant can mean considerable losses, firms tend to delay decisions as long as possible. So government aid and subsidies are used to encourage early investment, thus trying to avoid the 'stop/go' consequences.

The British government attempts to encourage competition by reinforcing legislation against monopolies and restrictive practices. Moreover, various Companies' Acts have been used to improve the quality of information provided in company accounts. Subsidies and incentives to industry are used to encourage a redistribution of industry, particularly in the development regions where resources lie fallow.

The growth in trading and the further development of industry and commerce necessitates the parallel expansion of services such as telecommunications, motorways, and port and harbour facilities. It is the government's adopted task to provide the satisfactory coordination of these needs.

Economic planning

Businesses have always planned in some way, and today this is almost a necessity. The increasing concentration of industrial units, resulting in a greater average unit size, has meant increasing complexity in decision-making. No longer is it possible in a big organisation for one man to absorb all the necessary intimate operational details of the enterprise and to exercise judgment on matters of the future. Decisions are not only complex, they often involve considerable sums of money, and influences may run for long periods well into the future. As companies now operate internationally, the complexity of operation is increased. So if resources are to be used efficiently and effectively, well-formulated specific plans are necessary.

Another significant justification for forward planning is in the increasing tempo of the rate of change – innovations in technology and socioeconomic sectors. The amount of money spent on research and development alone justifies planning of expenditure and the return on investment possibilities in terms of resource allocation.

This is considered so important that the use of staff specialists can be supported, for line staff tend to be concerned with today's problems and may not be able to adapt their thinking to future needs. Nevertheless, cooperation with line staff is essential, otherwise direct contact with the market will be lost and many real issues missed. Also, line staff are responsible for implementation, so their involvement is critical. However, the impetus for policy-forming aspects of planning are top management's responsibility, leaving the detailed features to operational management.

Long-range planning

The only observation about history that is irrefutable is that change has been certain. Adaptation to environmental conditions was the basis of Darwin's theory of natural selection. What is most startling in today's environment is the actual *rate* of change. This century has seen more change than has occurred before in the entire history of the world. Certainly we can predict that the future will be unlike the past, that it will escape all imaginative prophecies and that the velocity of change will continue to increase.

In management terms this means that skills will fall behind the development of techniques and that the techniques will drag behind the advance in the complexity of problems. The only way these problems can be met is by improvements in the quality of decision-making. And that means better data.

It means that critical decisions have to be identified and the minimum level of decision-making information determined, and that level will often be decided statistically according to probability theory, with the level of risk in each decision premeditated and chanced.

In addition, there is a need for productivity increases in marketing management, particularly in the selling of capital goods. Forceful marketing of plant and machinery should spark off further increases in the productivity of consumer goods, and a rise in the standard of living. Increased productivity in the marketing function presupposes advances in the utilisation of marketing resources, so a greater need for planning is proved. Consumer needs will grow, markets will continue to expand, purchasing power will inflate, and capital, social and political expenditure will continue to develop. The firms that will benefit will be those that see ahead, make plans and exploit the opportunities. Planning as a management activity is here to stay.

Demand forecasting

Demand or sales forecasting is the raw material of the marketing plan. The sales budget, and from it the marketing budget, are developed from the forecast, which is the key to the whole comprehensive budgeting and planning process. From the sales forecast the company develops a number of related forecasts, plans and budgets which determine production plans and inventory plans, and, as such, the level of business activity. In this way it provides the supporting sales data for the company profit objectives, the capital budget and operational financial planning, including the actual cash flow.

Demand forecasting operates at three distinct levels:

1 Macro-economic forecasts
2 Industry forecasts
3 Micro-economic forecasts

Macro-economic forecasting is concerned with general economic conditions. In the developed economies it is usually related to some tied indicator of industrial production or national income and expenditure. It is the area of demand in which the ruling government takes more than a passive interest. Governments also take an interest in the level of industrial demand. In the affluent countries it has been found that manipulating the fortunes of the car industry enables the politician to redirect the normal expenditure patterns of the population. For example, varying the initial deposit needed for a car purchase and changing the pay-back period enables the government to curb or stimulate consumer expenditure. By raising the value of the deposit and shortening the hire purchase period, the government slows down car consumption. As a result, the released disposable income each week is then spent on cash purchases such as clothes.

Intervention into the industrial evolutionary process is considered by many industrialists to be the root of British economic stagnation. By subsidising continuing investment in the old industries such as steel, coal and shipbuilding, the politicians have preserved votes but lost the opportunity to channel funds into those industries of the future, such as electronics, information, materials and leisure. It is no surprise that, with some notable exceptions, British industry finds it almost impossible to compete internationally in the competitively priced technological mass markets. The country may lead the world in the development and the production of major capital items such as turbines or nuclear reactors, but in the marketing of its produce it tends to lag behind, although more in reputation than in fact.

Demand or sales forecasting techniques
However, it is in forecasting at the level of the firm that the executive is mainly concerned. The forecast is a prediction of the level of sales activity if the circumstances remain unchanged, while the sales budget is the expected sales performance which the company sets as an objective. The budgeted figure may be set by management after allowance has been made for the effect of some additional factor over which the company can exercise influence, such as product quality or marketing expenditure.

The period for forecasts is wholly related to the lifespan of a product. Sales forecasts for repeat-selling consumer products such as frozen peas may only be prepared for one year ahead, in detail, while in shipbuilding a suitable period may be twenty years. But even this is not the whole truth, for in the world of fashion a particular style, as opposed to the garment itself, may survive for one short season only. Equally, a particular computer may be considered to provide a long period of service once installed, yet it may be obsolescent before installation is complete.

Short-term forecasting may often be undertaken using informed judgment and experience. Longer forecasts, often less liable to short fluctuations, lend themselves more readily to statistical projections. What does invalidate the universal acceptance of either method is the unpredictable nature of changing patterns of consumption. And therein lies the problem, for a demand function may only be possible if the sales determinants are constant, both during the period of observation and during the time of the forecast. For example, in short-term forecasting it is necessary to establish the conversion factors between determinants and the time-lag between each determinant as it functions.

(£000's)	Jan.	Feb.	Mar.	April	May	June	July
Enquiries	24	36	48	36	36	42	24
Quotes	20	20	30	40	30	40	35
Orders	20	10	10	15	20	15	20
Sales	12	16	8	8	12	16	12

In this example of an early warning device there is a time-lag of three months between receipt of an enquiry and completion of a sale. The conversion ratios are 6:5 enquiries/quotes; 2:1 quotes/orders; 5:4 orders/sales. In essence if enquiries in March fall to 24 and there is no discernible change in time-lag or in conversion ratios, then the company concerned may expect sales to drop to 8 in June, subject to any remedial action being taken as a result of the warning highlighted.

The problem facing most firms in compiling such a method is in the spread of activities. Too many products, too many markets and inadequate manpower prohibit adequate preparation of a forecast. The solution lies in isolating the significant products and the important markets – there will normally be few of these – and in preparing forecasts based on discernible trends and knowledge of market forces.

Developing the sales forecast

The method has many deviations inherent in its sequence, but some guide as to the steps necessary is essential.

Preliminary assessment

1 Level of profit assessment based on capital employed. How much profit is needed to meet obligations to shareholders and providers of loan capital?
2 The amount of sales volume needed to realise that profit figure.
3 The number and value of orders necessary for the sales volume to be achieved.
4 The number and value of quotations or tenders to be sent out in an effort to achieve the required level of orders.
5 The number and value of enquiries which have to be generated to provide for the quotations to be submitted.
6 The establishment of the conversion ratio or a trend in conversion ratio for each product group against required levels of profits, sales, orders, quotes and enquiries.
7 The measurement of the time-lag or a trend in the time-lag for each product group against required levels of profits etc.

This is a fairly simple method useful for the small business, which assumes that there is considerable market opportunity untapped. However, for the larger company this may not be realistic, because although it provides the manager with all the information he will need to develop his selling organisation it does not account for actual trends in the market place. In tackling this problem the manager has to use his best form of market feedback, the salesmen. Salesmen are usually asked to develop a sales forecast for their territory. The instructions given to them may involve the following steps:

1 Visit major accounts on territory (they probably account for 80% of his volume, although only 20% of his total customers at most) and get some positive idea of their future buying needs.

2 Check this information against recent data on buying and establish information consistent with trends.
3 Verify with customers where discrepancies arise.
4 With help of the manager apply confidence factors to each account forecast.
5 Remove from historical sales figures the actual volume achieved by these significant accounts.
6 Measure trends in the two separate sections.
7 Consider what action could improve the trends revealed.
8 What would it cost and is it worth it?
9 Arrive at figures consistent with trends in the market place and the costs of exploiting them.

Although these methods are the usual approaches adopted at the operational level, it is essential that the company prepares forecasts into the long term – not only for new products which themselves could alter the figures suggested by the sales force, but also for the development of new markets in anticipation of the decline of established markets. A staff officer would normally carry out such a procedure. He would evaluate prevailing and countervailing forces, such as:

1 Population trends
2 Developing living standards
3 Competition
4 World events
5 Government policies
6 Social values
7 Psychological needs
8 Fashions
9 Seasonal factors
10 Technological change

Following an evaluation of these factors, the staff officer is in a position to develop the information into demand determinants.

Demand determinants

This is a relatively elementary approach to the problem of forecasting, but discovering the influences on conversion ratios between determinants and related time-lags often provides invaluable insight into the workings of the company's demand function. Apart from the activities of the sales force (see Chapter 9), demand determinants are:

1 The number of actual and potential buyers
2 The available spending power of all buyers
3 The influence of price in the market place
4 The influence of pricing on substitutes
5 The distribution of spending power
6 The expectation of prosperity among consumers
7 The established reputation of suppliers
8 The structure of the industry

As reliable quantitative analysis cannot normally be extracted from this mix because it is constantly changing, it is therefore necessary to apply unsophisticated weightings to each determinant. These may be varied as time suggests. But in the end they are no more than indicative and should never be used as ultimate proof for a forecast. Establishing a trend may be taken as more reliable, but causation factors need to be appraised before conclusions are drawn.

Long-term forecasting

Statistical techniques such as time series or multiple regression analysis are most often used because they tend to eliminate the influences of short-term variations. However, these techniques cannot be used in an industry liable to sudden and rapid change. Such industries are those that are long established and traditional in outlook. One such industry in the UK is banking. Banks have moved into the home mortgage market, so changing the balance of their overall lending. Meantime the building societies are trying to have their basic roles changed so that they are able to provide a wider range of banking services.

The financial control of marketing planning

The common denominator of business is money. By using money as a yardstick it is possible to make comparisons of uncomparable activities. Whatever the social ethics involved, we compare a train driver responsible for hundreds of lives with a bookie by the amount of money society allows them. There is no direct comparison between their work, but we can compare them through the one factor common to them both – income, expressed in money terms. It may not be entirely satisfactory but it is workable.

This is also true in principle of marketing planning. No matter how unsatisfactory the system, we can compare relative values by the price society puts on them. So, despite assertions to the contrary, it is possible for the sales manager to prepare a comparison between recruiting a new salesman and spending more money on advertising. Once the common denominator is established it is then essential for the valuation of competing claims.

Marketing planning is in itself a financial control system. Suitably synthesised, the criterion is always: what is the return on investment consistent with the benefits of planning?

The benefits of marketing planning

Those companies that have successfully applied planning concepts have shown that the planning procedures involved lead to synergy: the practice brings greater total effectiveness than the sum of the separate parts would indicate. The major benefits at a company level are:

1 Considered judgment
2 Minimisation of capital requirements
3 Limiting of operating expenses
4 Optimisation of resources
5 Use of contribution analysis
6 Coordination of effort
7 Increasing personal responsibility
8 Internal competitive economies

These benefits are so important that some consideration of them is necessary.

1 Considered judgment
The only practical time to make unfavourable decisions is at a time of optimism when plans are first being made and tension is absent. Decisions forced on executives during periods of adverse trading

conditions often produce emotive directions. Planning well in advance helps to ensure well-balanced considered judgment.

2 Minimisation of capital requirements
While planning may help to make more effective use of plant and machinery, it is most likely to provide better financial management and so it limits unrealistic demands for capital to finance expansion.

3 Limiting of operating expenses
It may also help to reduce working capital by the reduction of stocks and the control of debtors' credit through cash-flow policies. It should help also to make marketing expenditure more productive.

4 Optimisation of resources
By aiding decision-making the planning process reduces the incidence of business risk and so helps to bring a better return on invested capital.

5 Use of contribution analysis
By analysing the business and its component activities it is possible to provide rudimentary product costings from which arbitrary profit figures per product and per unit of output may be calculated. Some companies load overheads onto these figures or put absorption rates against their direct costs. The resultant figures may be misleading (see Chapter 4 on product planning and pricing), so a profit contribution figure is most likely to be reliable.

6 Coordination of effect
In writing his part of the plan the executive manager will discuss his plans with colleagues to get the best results. In establishing the objectives and budgeting the marketing mix a coordinated campaign plan will result. As every executive will know the programme of his colleagues, he will be able to fit into the overall pattern of activity that much better.

7 Increasing personal responsibility
Because remedial decisions are made prior to the event it is possible for junior executives to implement the necessary action at a predetermined level of activity. This amounts to day-to-day delegation of

operational control, so making it possible for middle management to control significant management activities. In effect it is a substantial raising of the average level of responsibility in the firm.

8 Internal competitive economies

Individuals tend to associate themselves formally or informally with groups. Under sound management, employees endeavour to express their pride in collective achievement by attempting to improve on the performance of friends in other departments. Although these competitive activities may be beyond normal comparison, the common denominator of the budget provides the means by which measurement becomes possible.

The job of the planning manager

The planning manager is normally responsible to the marketing director for ensuring that the tasks of suggesting strategies of development, providing information, monitoring and recommending corrective courses of action for the company as a whole are successfully carried out. He will usually be responsible for the organisation of planning so that a basis for decision-making is possible. He will need to ensure a reservoir of knowledge is built up among his staff so that an appropriate perspective will evolve in operating departments. As these plans will need integration, it is essential that both planning and operational departments suggest ideas and act as a check on the contributions from others.

The person leading the planning department must be capable of operating at a level of abstraction. So he should have reached the stage of managerial maturity where he has the capacity to bear the uncertainty and anxiety of decision-making when the outcome is well into the future. He will thus have graduated from a performer to a thinker and planner. In order to make this transition satisfactorily he must have developed considerable marketing skills and be sufficiently numerate to apply quantitative techniques to planning problems.

Contingency planning

No matter how carefully a company may have planned, something will go wrong and objectives will not be achieved. Planning is no panacea for commercial and industrial ills, so while it will often highlight problems and help towards their resolution it will not eliminate them altogether. Plans are made by people and they will· make the plans according to their own judgment. This is often at fault. So the prudent introduce into the plan alternative courses of action. These will be in two sections. The first will contain the short-term action required to minimise or maximise possible consequences of deviations from plan, and the second the medium- to long-term action necessary to exploit the changed environment.

As it is not possible to predict exactly every likely significant event, the contingency plan will contain remedial actions against groups of consequences of unexpected occurrences. So the profit plan will show statements for 70%, 80%, 90%, 110% and 120% actual performances against budget, each of these statements showing operational detail and headcounts. Automatically, at the time a trend becomes apparent at any one of these levels, prepared action takes place. This action will be to counter the adverse or the favourable position. It is a standby until such time as the cause for the variance is investigated and established.

The object of this short-term action is twofold: it is to preserve net profit and to secure future net profit. As profit has a higher incidence in the last 15% to 20% of sales, after overheads have been covered and when costs have become marginal, it follows almost by definition that a drop in sales will cause a more than proportionate decrease in profits. So in many instances preservation of sales performances must be taken as high priority in a contingency plan. Moreover, at the time the plan is established, each executive will have applied a sensitivity analysis to each item sufficient to question its viability at each level of operation. To this analysis will be applied the manager's own confidence factor. Confidence factors are the levels of expectancy that the man responsible applies to his targets. The principle is similar to that applied by bookmakers, who issue odds as a representation of their and their customers' joint evaluation of a horse's prospects. In purely commercial terms it is practised by assurance companies, who value premiums as confidence factors against death at a particular age group.

The marketing plan is a document of the corporate mind. It brings together all the separate parts, coordinates individual aspirations, both tethers and motivates as necessary, and conditions the collective minds of the organisation into the channels chosen for it by its leaders. In a way it can be regarded as an autobiography written prior to the period of its corporate life.

In Chapters 14 and 15 the reader is provided with a ready reference to essential areas in planning. See also the author's book *How to Prepare a Marketing Plan* (3rd edition, The Gower Press, 1982).

6

Distribution in Marketing

The process of distribution is not confined to the physical transportation of goods from manufacturer to consumer. The means by which a manufacturer makes goods available to his markets is a fundamental part of marketing strategy. Traditionally, consumers buy their requirements from a retail outlet, relying on their own judgment and that of the retailer in order to obtain best value for their money. This is becoming less true since sources of supply open to the individual are constantly changing. There has been, over the years, a major revolution in the channels of distribution affecting many familiar products.

Instead of selling automatically to retailers via wholesalers, companies are now considering the alternative ways in which they may bring their products to the attention of the public, making it convenient for people to buy at the most economical price. Certainly it is in the choice of distribution and the control of distribution that many companies have established their marketing reputations. McDonalds Fast Foods, Honda motorcycles, Coca-Cola and Braun appliances are well-known examples.

Manufacturers that at one time could supply only to wholesalers now use other means of distribution, even where they actually compete with wholesalers, and even retailers, for business. Wholesalers have always bought in bulk from manufacturers, specialising in a particular trade and selling goods in convenient quantities to retailers within their locality. The wholesaler earns a profit through bulk purchasing and prompt payment. In return he warehouses goods until required, sells and delivers, turning goods over as rapidly as possible in order to maximise the return on his investment. The major advantage to the manufacturer of using a wholesaler is a reduction in his own distribution costs. Without the wholesaler it may be necessary to make hundreds of small-value deliveries to retailers. The manufacturer will need to keep account of such trade and collect debts. Because the wholesaler provides the same type of service to a number of manufacturers he can spread the cost of operating his service over a number of suppliers, so minimising the expense incurred. In practice those manufacturers that have carried out the wholesaling function themselves have not managed to economise in any way, and the only advantage in continuing to bypass the wholesaler is greater control over the selling effort. The main disadvantage of using wholesalers is that they have little incentive to promote the goods of any specific manufacturer.

The distributive trades

The structure of the retail industry is complex. Conventional outlets range from corner shops to large department stores and multiple retail chains. Smaller outlets are often one-man businesses, whereas the chain stores are usually public companies. Independent retailers specialise in highly personal service, often providing credit and free deliveries. They tend to carry small stocks of a wide variety of goods within their accepted trade and, of necessity, charge comparatively high prices. Their customers prefer the specialised and individual service they provide and are prepared to pay a premium price in order to get the service that suits their needs.

Discount stores are a relatively recent innovation, although the principle has been practised for many years in certain trades. In line with recent trends they provide a self-service operation with a minimum of personal customer service. Customers select the goods they want, pay cash and find their own transport. Discount stores are predominantly non-food outlets which rely on a high rate of stock turn. Their growth has accelerated since the elimination of resale price maintenance on almost all consumer goods.

In combating the power of supermarkets, independent retailers have grouped together to form voluntary chains. As a group they arrange with wholesalers, and sometimes with manufacturers, to purchase in bulk, each outlet agreeing to take a specific share of the goods ordered.

Wholesaling
Recent changes in distribution patterns have reduced the volume of trade handled by wholesalers relative to other distributors and other channels of distribution. The wholesaling function takes many forms. It may be a specialist one handling a wide range of goods within a confined market group, such as pharmaceutical goods, or a general wholesaler who will carry those goods with a required profit margin irrespective of any market segment. Despite their decline in importance – due primarily to the disappearance of so many corner shops and the arrival of self-service on a large scale – wholesalers still provide a vital distributive function. The firm will buy in bulk and sell in small units, so reducing the incidence of physical distribution costs to the manufacturer. The wholesaler carries stocks and so provides a better back-up service to retailers, enabling the manufacturer to concentrate on economic batch production. And because the concern wholesales a wide range of goods, meeting the retailer's every requirement, more economic use is made of transport resources. Furthermore, wholesalers provide working capital to retail outlets in extending credit. However, for the growing manufacturer, the passive selling approach often adopted by wholesalers is inadequate. So he has moved away from selling through wholesalers and now controls his own selling effort by going direct to retailers, and in some cases direct to the consumer or user.

Supermarkets
The supermarket is probably the most significant innovation in retailing that has taken place in the past thirty years. A self-service store of more than 2000 square feet with a minimum of three check-out points, the supermarket specialises in the repeat selling of goods that are advertised nationally and for which there is a high regular demand. Because operators buy direct from manufacturers they are able to offer goods at low prices and to use cut prices and special offers to stimulate trade. Invariably they carry high fixed costs, and although the labour content is low, so is the profit margin per item sold. Thus supermarkets tend to measure profitability in terms of £'s per square foot of space rather than per item, although

volume of sales for each product is an integral part of space costings.

More recent developments in self-service have come from hypermarkets and out-of-town shopping centres. Hypermarkets are giant supermarkets offering a full range of consumer durables and providing extensive parking facilities. Out-of-town shopping centres may be free-standing permanent structures or a collection, often running into hundreds, of stalls offering a wide range of goods.

Department stores
Department stores carry a wide variety of merchandise under one roof, usually on several floors of a building with specific departments handling particular groups of goods. There is a high standard of personal service, often with credit terms and delivery facilities. These stores insist on a high standard of personnel and compete with others through skilled buying and centralised management control.

Co-operative societies
Co-operative societies have long been established and work on the principle of customer ownership. The stores provide goods to members and non-members, the profits accruing at the year-end being distributed to members according to the value of purchases during the period. The structure of co-operatives may resemble any of the other types of competing outlet, although the limited range of goods which many carry is often considered a deterrent to potential shoppers. A significant proportion of each society's purchases come from the Co-operative Wholesale Society, which tends to standardise on goods supplied, so limiting the individual appeal in any one area of store.

Multiple shops
Multiple shops are normally groups under central control which specialise in a particular class of products. Because they deal in a small range of goods they are able to respond quickly to changes in taste and fashion. They tend to standardise in their product ranges and offer goods at reasonable prices. Normally buying in bulk, they have been able to integrate the retail and wholesale functions. More recently, they have become increasingly owned by manufacturers, who use them as a captive outlet for their own merchandise.

Variety chain stores
Variety chain stores operate in a similar way to multiples but are not restricted to a small range of goods. They operate closely with manufacturers and are able to utilise the economies of scale.

Self-service concepts
The traditional outlets have been increasingly attacked by entirely new concepts in retailing. The self-service concept is now spreading through many non-food outlets. It is being met increasingly in garages; and the garages themselves are meeting competition from specialist stockists for major items in car-consumables such as tyres, batteries and exhaust systems. Other specialist shops such as fashion boutiques and health food stores are now commonplace. The Mothercare chain is today almost a national network in the UK.

Franchising
Franchise marketing operations are a feature of a large number of shopping centres. The Wimpy Bar and Kentucky Fried Chicken are well established and are providing services that did not exist in the same way previously. They are based on the marketing distribution concept traditionally used in public houses and, in this century, in petrol filling stations.

Some retail outlets have evolved because increased demand has not been satisfactorily met by traditional means. For instance, travel agents, earning discounts provided by tour operators, airlines and transport companies, make full arrangements for the traveller, giving advice on routes, accommodation and amenities. Likewise, money shops have appeared, providing 'instant' funds to credit-worthy customers.

Even the multiples have adjusted to demand in the High Street. Many of the long-established chains such as Marks & Spencer and British Home Stores now provide food counters. Some supermarkets have hit back by providing self-service clothing and accessories departments. The Home and Wear section of Tesco is an example.

Own-labels
Self-service and demand-pull advertising has swung selling power away from the retailer into the hands of the manufacturer. While the retailer needs to develop outlet loyalty in his locality, the

manufacturer wants to establish brand loyalty irrespective of outlet. Advertising to the home and self-selection methods benefit the manufacturer in the balance-of-power struggle. In an effort to combat the strength of the manufacturer at the point of sale, retailers have introduced their own brands, obtaining quality products from reliable manufacturers and selling them under the reputation they themselves have built up as retailers. There is no better example than St Michael of Marks & Spencer Plc.

In line with the changes in actual structure of retail selling are new methods of distribution for established products. In some cases traditional channels have been used for entirely different goods. Van selling has long been established for such products as milk and coal; yet today bread is delivered door to door along with soft drinks and is carried by vans operated by the milkman. A substantial portion of ice-cream sales now appear to be made through mobile ice-cream vans. Every child knows the meaning of those ubiquitous chimes. More recently, mobile fish-and-chip friers have appeared and, judging by the trade they seem to be generating, are here to stay. Vending machines are now being used for such diverse products as cosmetics, books and ready-packed meals, in conjunction with microwave ovens.

Direct selling, door-to-door, has long been a feature of community living. In recent years the scope has gone far beyond the traditional household brushes or the encyclopaedia hawkers. Most consumer durables have now been offered across the doorstep, and selling carpeting direct to the home has become as acceptable as the selling of insurance.

Direct response advertising has become a significant channel of both communication and distribution. Advertising in the press, particularly in the Sunday Colour Supplements, inviting orders through the post has brought new skills in creative advertising. Currently, the commercial television companies are entering into this field although it has so far been restricted largely to record albums and cassettes.

Party-plan selling
The original party-plan type of selling started, or at least pioneered, by Tupperware has progressed and now includes the sale of such

products as wigs, jewellery and children's clothing. The agent encourages housewives to throw tea parties for friends, so providing the agent with the opportunity to demonstrate her wares and win orders.

Mail order

Equally significant in terms of impact but with a much higher degree of penetration into the consumer area is mail order. There are a number of reasons for the rapid growth of this form of distribution, notably convenience, economy, credit, better buying information, privacy and the provision for returning unsuitable goods. These are all inherent in the marketing plan of companies that specialise in selling through mail order.

Shopping at leisure during any convenient moment or whilst relaxing, without having to travel around a shopping centre and being able to compare competing commodities from adequate information summarised in the catalogue, is now a trading method welcomed throughout society, particularly by young mothers or working wives. In many cases customers have become dedicated 'window shoppers', thumbing through catalogues and developing ideas about future requirements. The system has allowed the consumer to have almost the equivalent of a department store in the home.

Causes of changes in distribution methods

In the development of a marketing plan a decision has to be made as to how customers are to be serviced. For example, in distributing a trade magazine it would be necessary to define the type and the number of readers required. So a profile would be developed of the desired reader and an effort made to ascertain the number in existence. Most often this problem is one for the manufacturer. The service organisations and the distributive trades have developed along traditional lines and their channels tend to be firmly established. And this is the main danger to such organisations, for during the past decade the changes in retail distributions have been such that a radical upheaval in retail trade management is necessary.

These changes are being brought about by three trends. First, the costs of distribution are increasing at a higher rate than ever before.

And product-line policies involve an increasing variety of choices open to the consumer, while the consumer himself is experiencing a fundamental change in personal habits and social behaviour.

The costs of distribution have been a constant source of worry to economists and politicians alike for many years. It was said of the nineteenth century that its merchants had solved the problems of production and left the problems of distribution to the twentieth century. In effect this is true, for the industrial revolution provided the basis for today's mass-production techniques; yet these techniques are valueless in themselves unless the goods so produced can be sold. And therein lies the problem. Machines can be developed which operate at high speed and low cost, so reducing the unit production cost for their output. Yet distributing and selling is not easily subjected to automation. In fact, the tendency has always been towards artistic qualities in the marketing sphere, with a minimum of scientific application. In practical terms it seems that the initial output from a machine is comparatively easy to sell because it is bought by the well-to-do who would have been prepared to pay more. But as output is increased it is sold to people with a lower and lower level of funds and less propensity to buy. Each successful sale requires a marginally higher marketing cost, up to the point where incremental revenue equals incremental cost – the point of optimum profit. Now, in effect, this often means that the cost of distribution rises with the economies of scale, and it may eventually exceed the production and materials costs of the product. Yet if the distribution costs had not been incurred, the high level of sales would not have been achieved and the costs of manufacture could have been substantially higher, even to the point where they exceeded the combined costs of manufacture and distribution achieved when sold in volume and where incremental costs equalled incremental revenue.

One of the complaints frequently heard against the use of mass-production techniques is the elimination of choice that this involves. Well, clearly if mass marketing means mass production and together they mean goods at a price that can be afforded by all, then the elimination of choice for the minority may be a price worth paying, if in fact this were true. It is not, for the increasing variety of goods being made available is such that additional distribution costs have resulted.

Once mass markets have been established it becomes necessary for production to be increasingly concentrated at fewer and fewer locations. This standardisation of production points has two effects. First, it means that mass production can be achieved for a significant part of the total manufacturing process, so allowing an infinite variety of choice at the final assembly stage; and, secondly, it removes production from the immediate locality of markets and hence increases the physical distribution costs. And because of the considerable variety of completed goods held in stock by distributors and the administration costs of that stock handling, the channel distribution costs have increased as well.

In addition to this improvement in the variety of goods must be considered the extent to which the provision of convenience foods has increased distribution costs. Frozen foods have to be carried in refrigerated lorries and warehoused in cold-storage plants, and at the point of purchase they need a refrigerated display cabinet – all costs of distribution. Convenience foods provide an 'added value' to customers and this in itself is part of the service which has to be paid for in the distributive process.

But perhaps the most significant change in contributory factors has taken place in the market place itself. Modern society is living in an era of abundance; there is no real shortage of supply. Indeed, there is a surplus capacity in most countries, hence the unemployment figures. It has all come from productivity due to mass demand. And because there is no shortage the standard of living is high and relative values change. The shift towards leisure pursuits has ensured new markets for new industries and new markets for old industries. Time-saving and labour-saving devices and the elimination of drudgery and monotony in the domestic scene have altered the entire face of the average consumer. In fact, changes in the distribution of wealth have caused a major upheaval in the levels of demand and in the distributive channels that service them.

The organisation of distribution

In developing his organisation for marketing, the executive concerned must consider the type of outlet that will provide the selling point to the ultimate customer. For example, in selling books the publisher may choose a direct selling approach, with sales people calling at prospective customers' homes. Or he may decide on a vending machine sited at a railway station. Similarly, his choice may range through booksellers, mail order firms or book clubs. He may even elect to have his books distributed by a special class of outlet, such as a hairdresser, a boutique or a chemist's. This decision-making process is also true of the industrial equipment company, which makes a similar evaluation of alternatives.

In his assessment the executive will consider a number of influential factors. For instance, if he uses an agent in an overseas territory and decides to evaluate a possible alternative, such as establishing a branch office with his own employees, he will need to consider the conflicting merits of the following:

1 Product technicalities
2 Local channels of distribution
3 The actual market size and potential
4 The level of service needed
5 The after-sales service provided
6 Language problems
7 Nationalistic attitudes
8 Size and geography of territory
9 Availability of staff
10 Competitive pressures
11 Distance from headquarters
12 Cooperation of agent
13 Government regulations
14 Identifying consumers
15 Operating costs

Although from the manufacturer's point of view the major considerations in distribution are time and cost, the long-term development of a business is often a short-term problem. Detailed consideration of these commercial factors is, therefore, of paramount importance.

1 Product technicalities
Highly technical products tend to be sold by qualified technicians. While it is often enough for the seller to understand customer benefits, it is sometimes difficult for an unqualified man to win the confidence of a buyer, who invariably will be technically skilled. So

instead of teaching salesmen to emphasise product qualities and to understand market needs, employers take the easy route and hire the engineer or the pharmacist according to the product characteristics. In a market area where this practice is common the employer will want to know the extent to which he is conforming or pioneering in his approach.

2   Local channels of distribution

Who you know, not what you know, is a value factor. Certain people, either through industry or through flair, have established valuable connections within particular trades. They may not be particularly knowledgeable but their contacts have confidence in them, usually built up over a long period, and their loyalty to such people amounts almost to restrictive practices. Yet this should be regarded by the manufacturer as 'brand loyalty' involving a certain degree of monopoly in the market place.

Such people and organisations are common in the distributive trades, and it takes great courage and foresight to bypass 'the trade'. It is certainly not desirable unless one is in a position to operate from strength. Internationally known and accepted products often carve their own path, under appropriate guidance, through trade channels. But knowing the existing channels of distribution is critical, whether one chooses to use them or not.

3   Market size and potential

Although there is much to be gained from entering an established and sizeable market, equally there are advantages in aiming at markets with growth potential. In an established market there will be much information available about prospects and needs. Equally, the demand will be matured and the selling activity devoted to influencing the selected alternatives, rather than to educating the market and building up demand. But an untapped market gives rapid growth opportunities from early penetration, often resulting in buyer loyalty.

Ideally, one should select a market with growth potential which seems to have reached a high-level plateau yet is still waiting to take off. Examples in the UK during the early 1980s appear to be home electronics and information technology.

4 The level of service needed

Although many products are sold over the counter, there are just as many that are custom-built and require installation and servicing prior to use. This is certainly true of many consumer durables and almost invariably true of capital equipment. In either case there may be a need for demonstration or even instruction to users on the efficient use of the appliance. The level of service and the technical knowledge necessary to carry out that service will often dictate the type of organisation most suitable for the task.

5 After-sales service

Similarly, complex equipment needs regular maintenance and service, together with easily available spare parts. Many organisations have built up their business through using superior sales service and after-sales service as their major marketing strategy. The most notable example is provided by Rank Xerox, which introduced minimum standards of performance for its distributors as well as conformity in service standards for its agents' mechanics. As yet, after-sales service is under-utilised as a pre-order promotional activity at a corporate level. Yet salesmen often use the back-up service as a selling tool. It is perhaps unfortunate that many companies give a low priority to this aspect of their operation and thus are unwilling to draw attention to it. Companies have great opportunities to win business by improvements in this area.

6 Language problems

Communications between indigenous members of a population are difficult enough without the added complication of foreign languages. Yet foreign trade is a fact of life, and as no international language is totally acceptable it is up to the supplier to adapt to the needs of his customers and so speak their language.

While this is desirable at the personal level it is absolutely essential in literature, whether letters or promotional brochures. People do not buy something they do not understand and they will not accept an oral representation of a leaflet any more than you, the reader, would.

In countries where English, German or French is the native tongue the problem is usually easily surmountable. However, other languages do present obstacles, and unless bilingual specialists can be recruited it is often better to use specialist organisations rather than to set up a branch or a subsidiary.

7 Nationalistic attitudes

Many communities are uncompromisingly patriotic and refuse to consider any foreign alternatives to home-produced goods no matter how inferior the local goods may be. Between two different countries with common boundaries there may even be open hostility through centuries of dispute over territorial lines. Often an industry becomes almost totally dependent on another country for sales of its produce.

The UK itself has a dependence on Spain for the survival of its travel industry. The inclusive tour operators rely on Spain for a large percentage of their business. If Spain were to close its doors to the UK, for example over Gibraltar, then the industry in this country might well collapse almost overnight for a period. Spain would not suffer to the same extent because its surplus could well be taken up by the German and French tourists, all with unrestricted opportunity to enter the country.

Exporters from the UK have to be particularly careful, because so many overseas countries have attitudes towards the British running back many centuries.

8 Size and geography of territory

Belgium is often chosen by the world's exporters as the test market for overseas marketing. The country is geographically small and 25% of its population is located in the four cities of Antwerp, Brussels, Liege and Ghent.

Other countries, however, are not so easily penetrated. Geographically, some countries are impossible to tackle in one go. Ayala Sales Ltd built up its European business before tackling the logical, yet enormous, market in the Middle East.

The terrain of some countries may prove a deterrent. Even in Europe there are some countries considered inaccessible. Communications in parts of Wales and Scotland are considered almost non-existent, while access or egress in Norway is impossible for much of the year.

9 Availability of staff
Most countries have their unemployed, yet the very skills most needed by the trader will be universally demanded and the availability of such persons strictly limited.

Often it is better to take the necessary personnel into the country, where entry and work permits are possible, although this creates the language or nationalistic problem already mentioned.

10 Competitive pressures
The competition in every country will have decided its own marketing strategy, either as a result of a purposeful marketing plan or through expediency. The success or otherwise of these policies could be indicative of trends in the organisational structure of the distributive system native to the country concerned. Knowing the pricing policies of competitors enables a company to decide on its own entry point in the market and how much may have to be made available for distribution.

It is by assessing the needs of the market and by studying how the market is being served that a company carries out its 'gap analysis' and discovers just where the greatest potential is for its own approach.

The company may choose to isolate and to weight the bases of purchasing decisions by consumers or users. Normally a decision will involve consideration of:

(*a*)   Price
(*b*)   Technical specification
(*c*)   Delivery and supporting services
(*d*)   Packaging or packing
(*e*)   Company reputation
(*f*)   Product or service reputation
(*g*)   Personal connection

The technical specification will include the quality and performance of the item concerned.

11 Distance from headquarters
One of the many disadvantages of using distributors is loss of effective control of the marketing effort. Distributors take on a product and, as often as not, hope it will catch on during the course

of their normal promotional activities. If it does, then it may get more attention. If it does not, then it will be allowed to stagnate. Usually the product will get as much attention as the manufacturer demands and ensures of the distributor. This may often prove expensive in executive travel time.

Even in establishing a subsidiary or a branch office, it is essential to organise a proper monitoring system. Seeking regular reports, preferably according to a fixed schedule with predetermined reporting activities, is a vital means of effective control. Usually the further a branch is away from the head office, the more difficult it is to exercise such control.

So introducing and maintaining a full reporting system helps to ensure that the new venture grows up in the company image rather than as a wayward maverick.

12 Cooperation of agent

Often a reorganisation means loss of earnings to an agent. The manufacturer should recognise that this probability is not likely to excite the fullest cooperation when new plans are afoot.

If the cooperation of an agent is sought, and it is usually essential prior to the establishment of a local branch, then these services should be paid for in some way, even to the point of allowing the agent some future commission for his assistance. It needs to be recognised that, apart from simply bringing in orders, in the past the agent has been building up a business connection and that future sales may often be dependent on the foundations laid by the distributor. He may be equally useful in the future.

13 Government regulations

Apart from import restrictions, the biggest problem facing an importer will be in the safety regulations in the country of destination. The best source of information in the UK on this problem is THE – Technical Help for Exporters.

14 Identifying the consumer

If direct customer contact has always been left to the distributor it is not always easy for the manufacturer to develop a profile which will enable him to maintain his own direct contact in the market.

Agents are aware that successful importers may soon establish themselves in a growth market and that it is not always in their interest to reveal the secrets of their success or to allow the supplier access to customer lists. Knowing the customer enables the company to set up a suitable sales force and to develop a relevant advertising campaign using appropriate media.

15 Operating costs
This is easily the area most fraught with difficulty. Few companies really know just how much these costs are. The only way in which one can judge the feasibility of any distributive channel is by estimating profit contributions against likely volume. Because of the number of variables involved, a considerable degree of guesswork is inevitable no matter how sophisticated the accounting approach.

Often in practice it makes more sense for an importer to take over local companies, so ensuring that many of the initial induction problems are avoided.

Pricing decisions

Many manufacturers use a mixture of distribution channels. In some areas of the country they may sell direct to retailers, but in other areas where volume is low they are content to supply to one wholesaler. Similarly, in some channels it is worth while selling to a specialist wholesaler so as to get the most efficient national coverage. Furthermore, it often pays to let a rival concern have supplies of a product and to allow them to market it under their own brand name. Some manufacturers sell a product under two distinct names, one being sold through one channel and the other through another. Manufacturers use these manoeuvres not merely to achieve extra volume or market share but because they are often able to inflict discrimination on prices or on discounts according to different channels.

Mass marketing, the offspring of distribution

One of the early attempts at effective distribution was created in the mid-nineteenth century with the birth of the co-operative movement. Today the movement is one of the largest, if not the most successful, of the distribution networks. But the basic idea behind the Co-operative Society is essentially a marketing concept. As a national organisation based on the original principle of shopkeeper/ manufacturer it soon evolved into a manufacturer/wholesaler/ branch shop network, just as we know it today. The principle of good value for money aimed at mass markets precipitated mass marketing in order to sell the bulk supplies bought at low prices.

Physical distribution

All forms of transport are used to transfer man or materials from one point to another. To have immediate access to a product improves its value. Transport provides access and therefore increases the value of goods to society. In this sense it is wrong to look on transportation merely as a cost, for in truth it is adding value to goods by improving their marketability. This improvement in the value of goods is just as important to the purchaser as would be an improvement in design or an increase in quantity. Fast, inexpensive and efficient transport provides one of the critical elements in the development of communications and hence the advancement of marketing processes during the past hundred years or so. A transport network is one of the predominant features of all developed societies and is one of the first priorities undertaken by all developing nations in the promotion of trade.

Effective transport is a vital part of modern affluence and productivity. The economies of scale would be impossible without the means of distributing goods throughout the length and breadth of the land where they are demanded. The major areas of consumption, the big cities, would not have evolved without transport. No city as big as London could possibly survive from its own output. The UK itself is a substantial importer of its foodstuffs and could not last for more than a few months without imports.

7

Publicity

Advertising is a distinguishing feature prominent in the everyday lives of people in a free economy. Advertising is a marketing tool which aims to gain attention and to be noticed. And because it does this so successfully and is so widespread, it is frequently considered the most powerful of the marketing activities. While it is true that advertising is powerful, it is nonetheless no more than a significant element in the marketing of a product, for marketing is a fully integrated discipline requiring a purposeful blend of marketing activities. Thus advertising may on occasion be the most powerful tool but only to achieve a predetermined objective or objectives within the framework of a coordinated campaign. As such it is complementary to other marketing tools. The actual blend of the marketing mix and part played by advertising has been given some consideration in Chapter 2.

Most non-marketing executives will be aware of the impact of advertising in the marketing of branded consumer goods because they, as consumers, constitute critical market targets, according to their spending power, and as such figure prominently in the promotional plans of some advertisers. Yet in their everyday business activities they tend to be isolated from the attention of the suppliers of goods and survices. So they have little awareness of the advertising strategies employed by these promoters.

Repeat selling consumer goods

Advertising is a key promotional aid in the selling of goods that have a low unit price and are subject to frequent and constant consumption. Examples are foods, household necessities such as soap and detergents, toilet and cosmetic preparations, proprietary medicines and, until recently, cigarettes and tobacco. The principles involved in the marketing of these goods are relevant, however, to consumer durables and to industrial goods and services.

There are over eighteen million households in the UK and many hundreds of millions more in overseas markets. Multi-national companies with scope for mass markets throughout the world need to ensure that markets in the industrially developed countries provide the sustained growth in demand and tempo which makes mass production and further development viable. To achieve this aim the producer must communicate with his customer through advertising. He must advertise continuously in order to win the confidence and cooperation of the trade, and the support of customers. The consuming public is daily making choices and so advertisers are concerned with an *ever-changing share of an ever-changing market*. So to ensure that changes are to their advantage, advertisers must keep their names in front of the public. They must advertise regularly. The central themes behind every campaign must be *concentration*, *repetition*, and *domination*.

In order to sell successfully a product must give the consumer real satisfaction. It can only do this if it is good value for money, at least in the minds of the chosen market. So marketing men aim to obtain consumer goodwill. This brand loyalty, as it becomes, is built up from regular purchases. The function of advertising is to state the case for the product, to persuade people to try it and to remind those who have already tried it that it is there to be bought again. Products are therefore branded or carry the manufacturer's trade mark. This helps to ensure that a product is easily recognisable. It also brings to satisfied customers a form of guarantee that a further purchase will be of the same quality as the earlier one.

Many a product has been an established household word for many years. Often such products are heavily advertised. It may be concluded that such brands owe their success to advertising. Yet it would be more appropriate to say that advertising has brought the product to the attention of millions, over many years, and that as the product is still selling, and selling successfully, it has stood the test, repeatedly, of consumer satisfaction. It is not advertising that has made such products popular but the fact that they were sufficiently good to withstand critical market tests and thus make heavy expenditure on advertising worth while.

The services of an advertising agency

The very early advertising agencies were space salesmen, who sold their employer's advertising services by writing and designing clients' advertisements. These salesmen soon realised that advertisers needed more than one medium for their publicity, and so they became space brokers, earning commissions from the media-owners for placing advertisements. The commission system persists today, although it is often supplemented by service fees. The range of services offered by an agency, principally to make advertising campaigns more effective, is so comprehensive that commission, particularly on small budgets, does not cover the costs involved.

There are almost 1000 advertising agencies in the UK, of which a quarter are members of the Institute of Practitioners in Advertising. Agencies may consist of just a few highly skilled specialists or offer a total marketing service with hundreds of employees. A number of the larger agencies are able to undertake campaigns on an international scale, while smaller agencies often have good associations with a network of overseas agencies.

The primary function of the agency is to help the advertiser to sell his product as efficiently and as economically as possible. In order to do this the agency will suggest the appropriate use of media and will prepare campaign plans to achieve the company's objectives. But since advertising is only a part of the total promotional campaign, agencies need to make other services available for the use of clients. These services often include market research, packaging and display, merchandising and public relations. In recent years the agencies have formed separate operating companies to undertake these services. The administration and control is simplified in this way, particularly the question of payment.

Most advertising campaigns are no longer the result of inspired ideas created by brilliant individuals, although some creative hot-shops have established themselves and it must be admitted some recent campaigns have been successful due to creative flair. However, the modern campaign is plotted and planned with considerable accuracy. It is brought about by the study of media. The media planners collect and evaluate the wealth of information made available by newspapers, the trade and technical press, television companies, the academic world, research companies and HM Stationery Office. The media planners are trying to discover the best media to use for particular campaigns and how to get the best out of the money available. So the media planning department deals with the problems of using the client's advertising appropriation to convey his advertising message to the selected market segment and to make the most effective impact upon that chosen audience. The media buying department then converts this campaign plan into the actual purchase of advertising space and time.

Supplementing this activity is the creative department. The creativity of an agency may often prove to be its most outstanding feature, for the department contains artistic and literary services, providing suitable typography, artwork, copy and scripts.

The marketing department of an agency links closely with the client's own marketing department on such activities as pricing policies, trading terms, channel decisions, sales policies, market trends and competitive activity.

Deciding the advertising appropriation

Ideally, the advertising appropriation should be the minimum amount needed to achieve the company's marketing objectives. The objectives may relate to market share or to maintaining a premium price; they may even relate to establishing a chosen company image or perhaps to developing the total market for a product. It is the amount needed to achieve such objectives that dominates the total publicity budget, of which advertising plays a significant part. So the expenditure on advertising should be the most economical means of achieving the pre-set goals.

In practice the advertiser has a good idea of how much his advertising should cost for an established product. His experience of numerous campaigns, different media tried and various amounts of money expended will have given him, within narrow limits, a shrewd guide to the level of expenditure most suited to his needs. Perhaps one day a pre-set formula may become applicable, but the changing pattern of behaviour in consumer purchasing habits defies all attempts to establish criteria for evaluation. It is not possible to prophesy or to measure subsequently the effect advertising has on sales.

Launching a new product provides the advertisers with many almost insoluble problems: not only is the launch costly but also the risks are high. Before commercial television was introduced in the UK in 1956, a manufacturer had no means of carrying out a realistic test campaign in one area. Although he could use regional newspapers, the impact of national or Sunday papers would be missing. The area exercise would not therefore provide a sound indication of the success or otherwise of a national launch.

Although some national newspapers and consumer magazines offer split runs, they are not ideally matched to typical test areas. Publishing different editions in various parts of the country does however enable advertisers to have trials in smaller geographical markets before risking a national campaign. Regional newspapers are now more sophisticated and the Regional Newspaper Bureau provides considerable detail suitable for promotional purposes whatever the scale of operations required.

But commercial television with regional coverage made it possible for test marketing to be undertaken. An effective marketing campaign, with advertising appearing in regional media, can now be launched in a single area on a scale that is pro-rata to the possible expenditure in a national effort. Often success in one region encourages the company to undertake a major effort paid, as it were, out of the confidence accumulated in the initial test. But frequently the most important benefit from an area launch is the lessons learned.

Not all companies, however, decide their advertising appropriation in this way. The most common methods, often using expected sales revenue as a determinant, are:

1 Fixed percentage on past sales
2 Fixed percentage on expected sales
3 Competitive parity
4 Predicted surplus

Each of these alternatives, however, has particular advantages and disadvantages.

1   Fixed percentage on past sales

As past sales are the sole determinant, the expenditure has little or no relevance to the current needs. It is particularly questionable in markets subject to rapid change. Its major advantage is that the money has already been earned and the question of being able to afford the amount does not arise.

2   Fixed percentage on expected sales

The major advantage which may, but does not always, result from this method is the incentive to improve sales forecasting attempts. It also means that costs can be predicted according to sales volume and therefore controlled within tolerable limits. The system does have the fundamental disadvantage of discounting influential factors and it is therefore possible to accelerate a slump unnecessarily.

3   Competitive parity

The sole advantage of this method is that it may pre-empt a war between companies on the level of expenditure. The parity made would, however, have to have universal acceptance.

The system loses its relevance when it is considered that advertising is but one of the marketing tools and the blend of the marketing mix is unique to each company. Attempting to standardise on the rate of one element alone will cause distortion, for it will benefit some and injure others.

4   Predicted surplus

The system needs some explanation. A company calculates gross profit from its sales targets, deducts a satisfactory level of profit and then uses the surplus for advertising purposes.

While the system is an aid to profit orientation, it does pose problems as to what constitutes a satisfactory profit. It also means that where forecasts show a decline in revenue, unless advertising provides a boost, profit levels will almost certainly be maintained and advertising reduced.

Clearly none of these methods is entirely satisfactory, although the percentage to sales variation is probably the most often used. In the UK it has fluctuated around a national average of 3% of sales. All the methods described are dependent on the total advertising budget being set and then used as necessary. There is much justification for a new approach. Sales targets are set by sales region and based, ideally, on market sales potential. It should not be beyond the resources of the marketing man to build up a model for each territory using the same input as that employed in establishing sales targets aimed at achieving territorial objectives. These could then be totalled to arrive at the amount of the advertising appropriation. It is true that this presents problems in the UK, a country almost unique in its numerous national newspapers; but with the advent of commercial radio, allied to the growing influence of regional newspapers and free sheets, the possibility is real. Similar efforts could be applied to each brand or, perhaps, to each product group.

The advertising media

In overcoming marketing problems the advertiser may spend his advertising budget on either intensive or extensive coverage of markets. In an *intensive* campaign the objective is to reach a selected target audience repetitively. For an *extensive* campaign the objective is to reach as wide an audience as possible.

After deciding the particular product benefit or benefits, the target market, and the necessary advertising objective, the advertiser selects the most cost-effective media available. Examples of the available media for most consumer goods are commercial television, independent local radio, newspapers and magazines, cinema and posters. For the industrial marketing company the choice may be between magazines, direct mail or exhibitions. In both cases the aim will be to find the most effective medium to deliver the advertising message at the lowest cost. The emphasis here, however, is on cost effectiveness, not necessarily the lowest cost. Although the advertising media are in competition they should not be considered as being in direct competition. Each medium has its own characteristics, making direct quantitative comparisons difficult. Each medium also covers a different area of the total market and will be selected therefore according to the needs of the advertiser.

The essential parameters for media evaluation, selection and scheduling are those of impact, frequency, coverage and duration. *Impact* involves creative aspects, such as colour usage, size of space or length of commercial spot, the theme or novelty of the campaign. *Frequency* is the degree of repetitiveness required in the campaign to incite a favourable response, while *coverage* relates to the proportion of the total market it is considered necessary to reach. *Duration* involves the length and timing of the campaign, whether it be all the year round for toilet tissue, in January for summer holiday bookings, or in November and December for Christmas gifts. Ice cream may be advertised in summer months, yet soup may be featured in the winter.

Each of these four strategic factors requires a part of the advertising appropriation, and more spent on, say, coverage must be at the expense of one or more of the others. Each medium has its particular advantages and disadvantages relative to these strategic considerations, so decisions on media selection will often be determined by the marketing priorities involved.

Considerable research is undertaken and the findings made commercially available to help advertisers or their agencies make appropriate decisions. The Broadcasters Advertising Research Board (BARB) provides data on audience compositions for televison and radio, while the National Readership Survey (NRS) gives information on newspaper and magazine circulations and readership. British Rata and Data (BRAD) provides information on rate cards for the advertising media business, with Media Expenditure Analysis Ltd (MEAL) giving information on how much is spent and by whom. Target Group Index (TGI) publishes data on group classifications and consumer purchasing behaviour.

The practice of public relations

The practice of public relations goes far beyond the recognised business of press relations, exhibitions and seminars. Public relations are concerned with the development of company recognition due to its forthright policies and its frank and practical manner in dealing with the people within its environment. No matter how successful a company may be in dealing with and gaining support from the communications world, its public image will in the end depend on its true business attitude. Based on the modern proverb that 'actions speak louder than words', the company that enjoys sound public relations has made a conscious effort to build business relationships upon mutual trust and respect.

Many companies do not have a specialist public relations department. Yet their deeds will spread among those that have some vested interest in the firm's existence, whether they be suppliers or customers. This approach to a company's image, although modest and praiseworthy, is also regarded as passive. The modern attitude to business development requires an active effort to promote company achievements. In a world where many companies are flooding the communications media with newsworthy items, few reporters have the time to search out and record the performance of the modest.

All firms, no matter their size or number of employees, have a public image, ranging from the impressions gained from visiting salesmen to the view casual passers-by get of the premises. Images are created by actions as diverse as telephone-answering manners to road usage by identifiable company vehicles. Opinions of a company may be formed by visitors who have to avoid water and soap-suds on the shop floor or by friends and relations of past and present employees. It is in this area of public attitude that so many companies suffer from a poor public image, not simply because they ignore the opportunities available from the need of the media to fill their columns with interesting news and developments.

Public relations is often regarded by other business functions as the sweet that is handed out when medicine has to be taken. This can never be so. Good public relations have to be earned in the same way that a lasting marriage has to be earned. In an age where management techniques, attitudes and terminology are subject to constant innovation and change, it is difficult to keep the entire population abreast of individual company actions and their causation.

Although public relations and advertising use the same media (or at least the press relations part of public relations does, along with press and television advertising) they are in no way directly comparable activities and do not compete as business functions in any way. The two activities should be considered complementary as they both aim to achieve the same objective, but in very different ways. Public relations depends upon a statement of facts, creating a climate of goodwill by enhancing sales opportunities, expressions of company policy or objectives in order to ease recruitment or the raising of finance. It is an activity devoted to securing the cooperation of employees, customers, suppliers, shareholders, and potential employees and their families. It differs from advertising because its editorial or broadcasting coverage is not paid for, and therefore the information must rely on its newsworthy content in order to be given coverage by the media. The job of PR is to make news releases newsworthy.

Advertising, on the other hand, makes claims; it aims at direct sales. The material is of such potential importance to the advertiser that, in order to have it presented exactly the way he needs, he is prepared to pay for its appearance. As they appear in the advertisement columns these claims are clearly recognisable as claims made by the manufacturer for his own benefit, no matter how factual they may be.

So editorial coverage is probably the result of a continual PR campaign which has created sufficient interest for an editor to want to give all the facts to his readers. This achievement is rarely free, for the company concerned has had to devote resources to the PR function.

It is considered unwise to try to evaluate editorial coverage according to costs of advertisement space because:

(a) Editorial coverage is an expression of facts and therefore does not contain the same persuasive element that is characteristic of advertising.

(b) Editorial coverage carries more weight because it is considered to be more objective since it is what other people say about you, whereas advertising is quite clearly what you say about yourself.

(c) Editorial coverage is always subject to the availability of space and many, to the advertiser, valid points may be edited out and a balanced view (i.e. that most favourable to the advertiser) lost.

(d) Editorial coverage is not pre-tested for customer acceptability and it is possible that an unfortunate choice of word or expression may cause considerable damage, even with an otherwise favourable review.

However, without such explanations in terms meaningful to the population, company actions may be misunderstood and harmful interpretations placed upon company policy. A company that has fostered public awareness will have helped to build a 'confidence' bank, so that when the unexpected happens, such as a strike, public opinion may be favourable and more disposed to believe the announcements made by the management than those by other sources.

While most non-marketing executives are acquainted with the idea of public relations, few are acclimatised to the idea that the sole aim of a sound public relations policy is the creation of goodwill. Goodwill is regarded as being the value of the business, i.e. the price it could expect to bring on the market, less the realisable cost of assets such as land, plant and machinery. It is the premium that some other firm or individual is prepared to pay for the company as a going concern rather than as a stockpile of assets.

At one time a product or a business generated its own goodwill. But that was when goods available on the market were limited even for the well-to-do. Even then it would have been difficult for one firm to promote its image, for in the day of unbranded goods the reputation of the manufacturer was entirely in the hands of the retailer. At that time the retailer had almost the power of life or death over a firm. And this is still true today, despite the demise of so many corner shops, because the supermarket has assumed considerable power through the strength of its purse strings and through 'own-label' products. So while there was a gap for some thirty years or more in which the shop or store took a back seat – the days of the sellers' market – it is distribution that accounts for success in the consumer goods industry. It is often the esteem in which a firm is held, the image it has or has cultivated, that is the decisive factor. A persistent public relations policy should pay real dividends.

This is also true of industrial goods companies. Being reported favourably in the popular press, and having certain of its technical skills featured in the trade press, may often bring substantial benefits to the company. As with the service industries, where advertising is either forbidden or even uneconomic, suitable press commentary is an aid to the promotion of the facilities provided.

But where public relations really does make a difference is in differentiating one product from another. So the organisation that is able to instil confidence in the purchaser has the edge over the unknown firm. For the buyer is, in fact, purchasing the corporate 'personality' of the organisation inherent or embodied within the products it makes or supplies.

It is therefore vital to a company that everyone with whom it has dealings, whether they be shareholders, suppliers, employees, customers or the influential 'City', is favourable towards the company and its policies. No better example of good public relations is available than that of Marks & Spencers, with 'customer satisfaction guaranteed' and sound employee relations, or of Sainsburys with its 'value for money' reputation. The image of these companies has spread partly because of realistic management policies and partly because of the mediocre approach of so many of their competitors. But it has spread mainly because of the extensive distribution networks of the two organisations, which ensure that both companies' names and their policies become 'household' property. Normally a company has to employ a definite policy of promoting public relations, so building a 'confidence bank' among its markets by dispensing news currency at frequent intervals.

Two-way information flow

It is usually insufficient for a company merely to send out 'puffs' to the press, radio and television. It is necessary to obtain some feedback of the impact of company policies. To send out information and not to obtain public reaction is as valueless an exercise as reading a book and not understanding the words. So, in addition to informing the public about the organisation, the public relations function must present to the management of the firm an accurate, objective and balanced interpretation of public attitudes.

To do this the public relations practitioner develops an intelligence network and service which will attract input of all aspects of public opinion and attitudes. Moreover, to make his efforts fruitful, he provides for his clients the method and the means by which the current state of the environment in society's thinking may be tempered to suit both his clients' needs and his clients' customers' needs. Simply to tap the resources without directing them to the mutual benefit of both supplier and consumer is clearly not in the long-term best interests of manufacturers.

It follows from this observation that public relations as an activity is a direct reflection of the client it serves. A company that adopts lavish expenditure on public relations instead of pursuing sound commercial practices is doomed to failure even more quickly than might otherwise be so. For example, nothing incenses a customer more than seeing replicas of his unsatisfactory purchase praised, without foundation, in some trade journal. In response to a complaint the journal will soon redress the balance. The faulty practice will soon get its just deserts. The two-way flow of information is therefore beneficial to all deserving parties.

Public relations is a marketing function, reporting and advising a company on how to promote its public image. It exerts influence on management when policy decisions are being considered and implemented, and explains to its public the background to company decisions and reinforces positive marketing actions.

8

Marketing Communications

Sales promotion may be distinguished from advertising not only in actual practice but also in matters of emphasis. The major objective of all advertising effort is to persuade people of the advantages of ownership and of the profits its use will bring. Sales promotion is devoted to inciting people to buy, and to buy now. So sales promotion supplements the process of advertising by reminding people, often at the critical decision-making stage, of the benefits of an immediate purchase. Sales promotion activities therefore often take the form of an incentive, a short-term buying advantage.

Sales promotion is often identified as the activities 'below-the-line' in publicity, the 'line' being an undefined arbitrary division of expenditure on press advertising – the 'demand pull' – and on sales promotion -- the 'sales push'. Furthermore, it is because the line is ill-defined that dispute arises as to the true meaning of each term used – necessarily, because so many forms of publicity are in their infancy and, in reaching for maturity, the different activities tend to be interchangeable and dependent upon the influences of the firms that offer the services. They are in a constant state of flux. Hard definitions are soon challenged and found to be wanting.

Sales promotional methods

As sales promotion campaigns tend to be short-lived they are, almost by definition, used to solve short-term problems which are, nevertheless, ever-present. A sales campaign in a particular region, either related to a chosen product or aimed at a specific class of customer, is the ideal marketing problem for sales promotional activity. So although any one sales promotion idea is short-lived, it fits into the overall marketing programme as a short-term solution to a never-ending problem – sales performance and growth.

Sales promotion is often divided into three key areas:

1 Consumer promotions
2 Consumer pricing promotions
3 Permanent promotions

Consumer promotions and consumer pricing promotions both follow strictly the short-term emphasis of promotional activity, while permanent promotions quite clearly do not. Some further consideration of all three areas is advisable.

1 Consumer promotions
Although consumer promotions are often surprisingly effective in particular campaigns, they do tend to be the subject of a considerable backlash. Often one finds that a successful promotion precedes the product concerned being left off the shelves altogether. This may well suit those companies able to switch production facilities at short notice, or those that have found overstocking at some point in the distribution network and need to force goods through and build demand. It is not such a useful device for a company needing to boost its sales effort and hoping to win a long-term market share by such methods.

The normal consumer promotions are:

(a) Sampling – house to house with coupon
(b) Sampling – in-store plus coupon
(c) Coupons – through the door
(d) Coupons – through selected media
(e) Premium promotions (the daffodil)
(f) Bonus pack (extra portion)
(g) Money-off
(h) Self-liquidating offers

These techniques are often known as incentive marketing and have been a growth industry since the advent of television advertising, coupled with self-service, helped them to take off. They are all the result of volume sales – or, to be more precise, anticipated volume sales.

Sampling is without doubt the best method of launching a new product, but because of the often considerable expense involved few firms are prepared to risk the investment it demands. Yet, assuming the product to be good, sampling does allow trial and appreciation at each distribution level, since people are often glad of the opportunity to try a product before spending money. Sampling also has the advantage of exercising some influence over those people who would not normally experiment with new products. Sampling proves to be most effective when prospects are selected in advance and the approval, through sampling, of distributors is won, and particularly when some form of in-store demonstration runs concurrently with the sampling period. The most critical aspect of using samples is to ensure that the sample is an exact replica in pack and form of the product to be put on sale.

The provision of coupons is a price concession and at best no more than a substitute for sampling. As is usual in the business world, the usefulness of coupons declines in proportion to the amount of money spent on them.

Consumer promotions do, however, have a part to play in marketing tactics. Experience has shown the methods are best suited to:

(*a*) New products with a distinguishable product advantage
(*b*) Products in competitive growth
(*c*) Supplementary promotions

They are least effective:

(*a*) For established products, particularly if sales are declining
(*b*) When unsupported with other brand promotions.
(*c*) In an aura of constant pricing promotions.
(*d*) As a defensive measure in intense promotional competition

These conclusions are drawn from the conclusions and experiences of numerous promotional executives. Yet each of these executives is able to relate a case history where the conclusions were different from those stated above. This indicates that, as a general rule, the above conclusions are correct, but the inspired marketing man may well defy them and succeed. And that is true of any 'rule' of marketing management.

2 Consumer pricing promotions

Tactical pricing promotions tend to be the promotional method most often encountered, probably because it is the easiest to choose and often the simplest to justify. But it is frequently based on the often fallacious argument of high-volume low profit margins. Pricing promotions are best undertaken from positions of strength. Rarely do they work when things are going badly. If sales are growing and a pioneer or market leader wishes to expand the total market and/or to, win market share from a smaller competitor, then a pricing promotion can be very effective – but only for a short period of time. If continued for too long, the promotion will backlash on the manufacturer.

Sometimes an advertiser wishing to achieve wider distribution may embark on a pricing promotion while maintaining trade channel margins. This assists distribution, but only where the outlets anticipate increased sales. That often means the full support of an extensive promotional campaign.

The rules on tactical pricing are quite clear:

(*a*)   Consumers identify a price with value for money. They often resent prices returning to normal after an extensive campaign. They may switch to a competitive brand whose price has been maintained.
(*b*)   The flow of supply and demand often works when price promotional activity takes place.
(*c*)   Price promotions are most beneficial when offered as two packs for the price of one or, as suggested earlier, through couponing. Making a straight reduction often incites the consumer to stock up while the special offer is running. There are, in addition, a number of variations on consumer promotions and pricing, and these may often produce impetus to sales, particularly if the theme is being pioneered.

3 Permanent promotions

Such promotions are often critical to the success of certain product lines. Where demonstrations are essential to a purchase, such as with cars, then a permanent showroom has to be maintained. Just like promotions in supermarkets, showrooms need to follow certain rules. For example, a sports car or a convertible may attract a customer into the area, but because of family needs he will probably buy a saloon. However, he might never have entered the showroom if it were not for the sports car in the window.

Often, for instance in garden centres, the consumer is best attracted when he sees a product in its natural setting. This is why so many products on sale in stores have illustrated examples showing just what the buyer is capable of producing.

Clearly there are some products of which it is impossible for the salesman to carry samples or even for the typical store to make a display. Boats are an example. Yet boatsellers are canny; they try to avoid being too close to water, because otherwise selling becomes a matter of frequent demonstration and infrequent orders.

The mobile exhibition has become a feature of current promotional activity and offers cost benefits for companies where permanent exhibitions are essential to the main selling effort.

A technique now being used successfully by some companies is the permanent showroom in a department store or a retail chain shop. The company concerned hires space within the premises and takes advantage of the traffic flow of the store to provide sales opportunities. A number of travel agents are operating in this way, as are some suppliers of soft furnishings. For some years a number of cosmetic manufacturers have signed franchise agreements within such a framework.

Merchandising

Conclusive purchasing decisions are made at the point of sale, now increasingly referred to as the point of purchase. The part of sales promotion that provides the final impetus, reassures the prospect and makes it easy for him to buy has become known as merchandising. Among its practitioners it is known variously as the 'silent salesman' or as 'selling through' techniques.

It owes its present position in marketing to the advent of self-service. The depersonalisation of retail selling necessitated an alternative to the sales assistant – a system that performed the functions of the seller but without the costs involved. The system, in other words, had to sell. And because of competition at retail level the function of selling itself had become more critical.

Failure to put the product in the right place and at the right time frequently means no sale. Because the fight for shelf space grows more intense, the need for sales per square foot is critical. So the manufacturer must ensure that his sales performance matches the terms demanded by the retailer. The manufacturer, in fact, must now provide the means by which his product sells at the point of purchase. He has provided advertising. He has used sales promotion. And he must merchandise. To achieve this aim he uses specially trained salesmen, known as merchandisers, who are skilled in product display, store layout, and promotional techniques and production. Merchandisers are now commonly used in grocery, hardware and chemist's shops.

It is therefore clear that merchandising is the means by which a manufacturer and his retailer combine their resources in the common aim to increase sales. Obviously the other forms of publicity are an aid to the retailer, and in the case of coupons he actually assists the manufacturer in a promotion. But this is cooperation. Merchandising requires the guidance and promotional materials of the manufacturer – based on his selling strategy – and the facilities of the retailer. Yet the aims and goals of the two are different. The retailer's needs are:

1 To bring prospects into the shop
2 To increase store traffic (the circulation within the shop)
3 To sell a full range of products
4 To maintain shop loyalty
5 To increase average spending

It is clear from this that the retail outlet has little interest in individual products but is mainly concerned with maximising its asset, which is a *point of purchase*. So the retailer wants fast-moving goods with healthy profit margins. Sometimes the retailer will require help in announcing a new line or in selling off slow-moving goods. These are often the subject of a special offer. The needs of the manufacturer, however, are:

1 To ensure that distribution reaches the shelves

2   To obtain a prominent selling position
3   To provide product recognition
4   To provide shopper identification with the product

The manufacturer cannot achieve these objectives by using merchandising alone, for the technique is but an integral part of the marketing process. Without the full support of the marketing programme, merchandising may well be wasted.

Merchandising depends for its success on the discernible behaviour of the consumer. Although research findings are limited, some commonly accepted criteria have emerged. For example:

(a)   The prime selling spots are gondola ends, eye-level shelves and the checkout area. Children are vulnerable to confectionery carefully placed within their reach, and if the unit value is low mother will pay.

(b)   Shopping habits involve twenty minutes in a familiar supermarket and no shopping lists with the majority, although a clear idea of purchases needed is usual. The average shopper knows the location of pre-selected purchases and removal of particular goods is semi-automatic.

(c)   Decision-making is rarely a matter of conscious thought at the point of purchase. If not predetermined, then it becomes an irrational purchase, often through self-indulgence.

The activity of merchandising involves the layout of a store, the deployment of display material and the reflection of house style. But it is in the combination of these methods that merchandising is most effective. They need to be considered in some detail.

The layout of a store

It is the merchandiser's aim to provide a traffic flow situation in the shop that encourages a steady progression through the entire store but where each diversion carries an incentive to continue around the store. The store wants maximum exposure of its range to the highest possible number of shoppers. Often the slow-moving, less popular lines will be placed in prominent positions, for the fast-moving commodities will usually be searched for by brand-loyal shoppers. As consumers appear to shop in a daze, it is common practice to place dump bins in the centre of traffic lanes, so ensuring full attention as the housewife walks round them. Some merchandisers have to act as supervisors to shelf-fillers, many of whom are local housewives earning pin-money.

The deployment of display material

All stores receive more display material than they can usefully use. Competition for the limited space available for showcards, shelf-talkers, display cases, mobiles, swing tickets, headboards and many others is tough. So the material must not only *be* capable of moving products but must also *appear* capable of moving them. Frequently the decision as to what is to be used comes as a directive to the store from head office. It may often be the result of a central purchasing agreement. Increasingly the super stores and the voluntary chains are producing their own display material.

The reflection of house style

Certain retail chains have recognised the merchandising advantages of house style. Often house style is a direct reflection of the retailer's own marketing strategy. It is this development which has led to retailers providing their own display material. This is obtained to show the appropriate image for the store consistent with its need to attract the consumers it has chosen to serve. Promoting a house style is usual in other forms of publicity where collective impact exceeds what would probably have been achieved with separate advertisements. The house style promotion has developed with and parallel to the 'own label' package. In this case the retailer puts his own reputation at stake in branding a manufacturer's line with his own name.

Below-the-line publicity is now an expanding industry and is currently described as *incentive marketing*. Techniques are now more sophisticated, with some local newspapers carrying money-off vouchers for readers. Similarly video-recorders on rental entitling membership to video clubs, gifts provided by mail order firms to prospective agents, and cash refunds for specified numbers of purchases are current examples. Premium promotions still flourish and reduced price goods are still available after the accumulation of brand labels. The prize competition is perhaps the most prevalent and hundreds are in operation all the year round.

Packaging

Packaging has been an essential feature of the trading scene since man carried water or milk for sale. Today in the UK some 2–3% of the gross national product is spent on packaging materials. In the early days packaging was primarily used for security of the contents. In the case of gunpowder or corrosive materials, security was also needed for those who actually handled the goods.

But security is no longer the sole requirement, for packaging may incorporate considerable selling power and may often be used to establish identity, to provide information on its contents and their use, to suggest the care needed in handling and, significantly, to supplement the merchandising effort at the point of purchase. Packaging is therefore capable of being used as a powerful promotional medium. It is, in fact, increasingly becoming a full-bodied marketing communications channel.

Part of the progression from bulk packaging to unit packaging is attributable to the widespread adoption of branding. At the same time many local producers became uneconomic and production units were increasingly devoted to a few areas of a country, with output being distributed through fast-developing distribution networks. So the physical handling of goods over long distances, the exposure to the elements and the sheer time needed in transit created real needs for better packaging.

Modern packaging facilities mushroomed however, with the arrival of commercial television and the adoption of self-service trading. As in merchandising, the package assumed a vital role in the selling of the product at the point of purchase. Furthermore, because the product would be demonstrated on television – in its pack so that it could easily be identified – the need for superior packaging became clear, and with colour television firmly on the scene the need is intensified.

Today's consumer, it is said, lives in an era of abundance. To the psychologist many of the tensions of modern life are associated with the problems of choice. Present-day neurosis is often attributable, it seems, to the almost infinite variety of choices facing the shopper. To the manufacturer, however, it suggests the need for a positive approach to making it easy for the purchaser to buy. By providing easy recognition, clear benefits and an attraction in the packaging itself, the manufacturer exploits his opportunity, but in doing so he fulfils a felt need. In addition, the package can provide a unique promotional opportunity, for the advertising message on the pack may be seen after the purchase in the home every time the product is used. When stored, say, in the kitchen, its pack is a constant reminder to the housewife. Even when the pack is empty it provides a promotional activity – because it needs replacing.

Packaging as a marketing tool
Packaging is a critical part of the marketing mix and frequently appears as marketing strategy. If the product for sale is usually bought as a gift for someone else's consumption, then more money spent on the container than on the contents may be desirable. For example, some brands of cosmetics tend to sell on 'their appearance on the dressing table' rather than on their appearance on the face or body. Similarly, cutlery sets customarily bought as wedding presents may be more appealing to the purchaser if the package implies an expensive gift.

There are numerous variations on these strategic themes:

1 A new pack may provide an uncountered promotion.
2 A new pack may revitalise flagging sales.
3 A new pack may extend the product life cycle.
4 A new pack may revitalise the 'trade' interest.
5 Seasonal variations may be avoided by deep-freezing.
6 Packs may be designed for ease of handling.
7 Packs may be designed for economy in transit.
8 Costs may be reduced through packaging technology.
9 New markets may be entered through packaging technology.
10 Established markets may be reborn through packaging technology.

The major innovations in packaging in recent years seem to be in the use of plastic film, aerosol, frozen foods, dehydrated foods and prepared foods. The emphasis is as much on convenience as it is on the actual package, so a complete new service strategy has evolved from packaging principles. But packaging as a strategic weapon is not the complete story. The design of a package may be deliberately aimed at reducing pilferage, shop-lifting being a major problem in all classes of outlet. It also has a prime function to perform in ensuring the safety of the contents. Efforts must be made to prevent access of rodents if food is stored for any length of time, so should the migration of inks and glue be prevented. Equally important is the avoidance of loss through destruction or deterioration of the contents.

Packaging as a behavioural tool

In this era of mass production real product differences have almost disappeared. Packaging is a means by which the consumer is able to distinguish one product from another, either because it adds an extra service element or because it provides some psychological satisfaction. In a society that has enough to eat, adequate clothing and shelter, and almost all the material things of life, it is often the satisfaction of deep-rooted desires such as social acceptance, feelings of superiority, and freedom from fear and danger that give a product the edge it needs over competition. So packaging may give a product its unique selling proposition. In that sense, the package becomes indistinguishable from the product. 'Dimple' whisky, potato crisps, hairsprays, instant-bond glue where the package is also an applicator, and long-playing records are examples of products for which the package seems almost indispensable. Clearly there are some products where this is completely true, such as photographic film or medicines, but these are security measures rather than added value.

Colour is one of the most useful ploys in conveying psychological ideas about products. Perhaps it is a direct reflection of developed dress-sense or even a natural association taken from habitual usage. For example, white is known to convey impressions of cleanliness and purity. It is emphasised in detergents, it is the colour of the traditional wedding dress and it has long been a feature of hospitals, both in decor and in medical staff dress. Other colours and their associations are:

> Black – strong, overpowering
> Blue – cool, distinction
> Brown – utility, general
> Gold – royal, rich
> Green – natural, quiet
> Orange – warmth, mobility
> Purple – lush, extravagant

Red – hot, excitement
Yellow – warm, sunshine

Different shades of these colours may accentuate or soften the idea to be conveyed. For added emphasis a combination of colours may be used. Orange and black is frequently considered a highly sensuous combination, while green together with the two blues of Oxford and Cambridge (the colours used for the European Marketing Congress) convey modesty, coupled with intelligence and dynamism. So in the shopping centre, associations of ideas may create favourable or unfavourable buying habits. Colour can therefore be used to sell.

Direct mail

Although scorned by many, direct mail is probably the most versatile of all the advertising media, for it is the only medium that is capable of being matched with the individual requirements of any or of all advertisers. It can be directed economically at a few or effectively at many. The advertisement may be sophisticated or simple, as required by the advertiser. He is not obliged to use the accepted inflexible format usual in other media.

The two most constant criticisms of the technique are that there is a high wastage factor and that mailing lists soon become outdated. Each point is true. But these weaknesses are recognised, and can be measured and minimised. If the required success ratio for a mailing is 5% and a mailing list compiled over five years has a known success ratio of only 1%, then investigation of the mailing list will reveal different success ratios for each year of the five-year period. If the two most recent years have an average ratio of 10%, then it would be worth while undertaking a mailing to the addresses acquired during that period. No other form of advertising can combine selectivity and objectivity in this way.

Direct mail is so versatile that it can be used as a market research tool. Although it has some limitations when compared with telephone or field research, it does enable the researcher to operate more economically and it provides more opportunities for the informant to consider questions without haste and, where necessary, to obtain supporting information.

As a marketing tool the technique has much to commend it. For apart from this market research potential, the medium makes customer profile compilation possible and the end product realistic. These profiles may then be subjected to considerable analysis and should provide an investigator with the basic data essential to the development of a formula helpful in calculating a propensity to purchase.

The profiles will also prove useful in winning customer confidence. Because direct mail is, or at least should be, entirely personal it is possible for the advertiser to take advantage of the information contained within his profiles by emphasising some private detail or characteristic, so suggesting to the prospect a highly personal offer.

The benefits of direct mail

The benefits of direct mail are contained within its differences when compared with other media. These basic differences are:

1 It is selective.
2 It is confidential.
3 It is non-competitive.
4 It has flexibility.
5 It has originality.
6 It has no schedule.
7 It can be modulated.
8 It can be timed.
9 It can include action aids.
10 It provides feedback.

This is an impressive list of attributes considering the limited appreciation for the medium. But of course these benefits are not automatic, they come as a result of careful and considered use of the facilities available. Some detailed consideration of these benefits is therefore warranted.

1 It is selective. A direct mail shot may be sent to particular individuals or to groups of individuals in one market precisely, and therefore more economically than other media, and in particular to small or unusual sectors. There are firms that specialise in compiling such lists and often they will offer a guarantee as to the accuracy of their lists.

2   It is confidential. Only direct mail achieves complete confidentiality – if necessary. Because each mailing shot is addressed to a particular individual and may be sealed against alien eyes, it can convey messages of privacy or even those of an intimate nature.

3   It is non-competitive. Advertising has to battle with competing claims for attention. Commercial breaks on television may be used as natural breaks, while newspapers need a 60:40 ratio in favour of advertising to survive. Outdoor and transport advertising, posters and signs compete against the counter attractions of the real living world. But direct mail arriving in the post has the maximum possible chance of winning attention – it may even monopolise the breakfast table.

4   It has flexibility. Apart from postal regulations and the restrictions imposed by common sense and good taste, there is almost no limit to the size, shape or format for a direct mail shot. Similarly, there is extensive scope for the use of materials and productive processes.

5   It has originality. Because of the considerable flexibility in the styling of a direct mail shot, it is possible to incorporate a creative element in the advertising used, almost to the point of complete originality. Certainly there is scope for initiative or inspiration. This is particularly significant in a world of near homogeneity of available products.

6   It has no schedule. Unlike newspapers, magazines or television, where timing of publication or broadcast is essential, direct mail letters may be sent out at the convenience of the advertiser. Admittedly he is restricted to some extent by the work programme of his production department or of the mailing agency.

7   It can be modulated. Big things from small beginnings could almost be the motto for any mailing campaign. The advertiser may run his campaign regionally, using the returns from one area to subsidise his action in the next. He could divide the total market into product groups, or market segments, and build up business by tackling one part at a time.

8   It can be timed. Because direct mailing has no schedule other than that required by arrangement between the advertiser and the mailing house, it is possible for mailings to be made to suit any event or occasion. So launching a new product or giving support to a major campaign can be programmed as needed.

9   It can include action aids. Reply-paid postcards or order forms can be included, making it easier for the prospect to take action. Most marketing men are concerned with overcoming apathy and so any aid to solving that problem is welcomed.

10   It can provide measurement. Because the mailing list is pre-selected and the advertisement developed specially for that market, it is possible for the advertiser to monitor his results and so establish a rate of returns. In this way he is able to identify the profit performance of his advertising.

Direct mail shows every sign of becoming the medium of the future. Like the selling function, it needs only to establish a respectable image.

9

Selling and the Sales Force

Selling is the most dynamic force of marketing because it is the only activity that generates revenue – the life blood of a business organisation. It may be true that certain other activities are revenue-raising, such as advertising in a mail order operation, but invariably they are but a substitute for selling effort. Consider an advertisement in a newspaper inviting business through the post: it is an impersonal selling action. It is, in fact, using those parts of the selling operation that may be presented graphically. The other aspects of the selling process come later when the customer either approves or returns the goods delivered.

Selling has always been a part of trading, and trading has a history as long as civilisation. It was selling that made the division of labour possible, long before Adam Smith wrote about his pin-maker. But during the early days of trading, selling was preoccupied with satisfying existing demand by locating and identifying prospects and convincing them of the items' merits as compared, perhaps, with alternative purchasing opportunities. Today selling is equally involved with the development of a latent need into a positive demand.

The change in emphasis happened at the time of the Industrial Revolution. Historically, traders had their wares made in the cottage industry, similar to that prevailing today on the Isle of Lewis for the production of Harris Tweed. The turn to machines in the nineteenth century meant centralisation of production. It also meant a considerable increase in productivity. Previously, merchants had traded in local markets, while the more enterprising sent the surplus to the neighbouring big city. This was on a modest scale. Then suddenly with machines churning out unheard-of quantities, albeit at a low unit cost, it was essential for the merchant to tackle entirely new markets. Moreover, because of the volume involved, he was unable to perform the necessary selling function alone. So he hired salesmen to sell – to sell to people who had little knowledge of the utility of the products concerned. Now with the help of the salesman they had to be persuaded to change their attitudes and 'invest' in a better living. The cumulative effect was a phenomenal growth in demand, in production and in the standard of living. Therefore the stimulus for creating today's wealth among the industrially advanced nations has been a result of the selling process.

The art of communication

The practice of marketing is described in this book as common sense and the ability to communicate. Because common sense is comparatively rare and, like all human characteristics, is unequally divided between the personal faculties, pursuits and attitudes of the individual, true selling ability is uncommon. Besides which the problems of communication are such that they are probably responsible for the greater part of dissension between peoples throughout history. Yet the salesman was the original marketing package. All other marketing activities have evolved to supplement and, hopefully, complement his performance. So the practice of marketing and the benefits it brings to society originated in the salesman. In fact, the truly professional salesman has practised marketing doctrines for as long as the history of trading.

The salesman sets out to persuade. He persuades by concentrating on the satisfaction, or the prospect of satisfaction, of deep-rooted desires. The salesman is aware that people purchase benefits – what a product does for them – not just the product for its own sake. Often consumers are able to relate this logically in their own minds, for when a person buys a spade it is because he wants to dig a hole in the ground or needs to move something from one spot to another. A spade is the means by which he satisfies his need. It happens sometimes that the buyer is only partially aware of the purpose behind his or her purchase. Buying an expensive pen will allow the purchaser to write only marginally better, graphically, than he would with a cheap pen, but the pride of ownership, much of which may be latent, may be a positive reason for the extra cost. There are other occasions when the person has no real idea of why he or she has made a purchase. Buying a new hat which may never be worn is, possibly, a means of relieving 'pent-up' emotion. Many impulse purchases in supermarkets – selling through the silent salesman – originate, it is believed, because of self-indulgence, itself generated by boredom or by a desire to reject any form of discipline irrespective of whether it is self-imposed or otherwise. Salesmen learn to recognise the signals that the customer gives out, in much the same way that we in our social lives recognise the symptoms of boredom, anxiety, anger, frustration or excitement. It comes from a constant study of people.

Before we consider the fundamental desires inherent in the human personality it is necessary to see how the salesman uses his own knowledge of physical attributes to communicate. Basically, people communicate in two ways: knowingly and unknowingly. The professional salesman uses both. He uses the techniques of planned selling to communicate knowingly and the five, or perhaps six, senses to communicate 'unknowingly'. Let us consider unknowing communication first.

People judge others by what they experience on contact with them. They use their senses to do this:

1 Sight
2 Sound
3 Touch
4 Taste
5 Smell

The salesman takes great care to provide better than acceptable standards in the normal sense. He will also continue to use his understanding of these 'sense judgments' to communicate. By the use of these senses he communicates enthusiasm, sincerity, drive, interest, understanding, earnestness, consideration, integrity, knowledge and industriousness. The list is not exhaustive. Study of the classified columns of The *Daily Telegraph* will produce a never-ending list of essential selling characteristics. In selling it is not enough to be merely good, it is necessary, modestly of course, to show it. And it wins the confidence of customers and produces orders.

Nevertheless, the wise salesman does not stop at personal communication of this sort. In addition, he provides sales aids to reinforce his own personality and to provide further communication opportunities.

Exploiting innate desires

Selling people what they really need is not only a marketing philosophy but also a psychological appeal to their deep-rooted desires. Psychologists compare the human personality to the iceberg. Man allows but a part of his total personality to be revealed, leaving the greater portion beneath the surface, hidden from all but those closest to him. So he remains unmoved by the surface winds, no matter how strongly they blow. He will, however, tend to move with deep ocean currents as they play against his great bulk below the surface. For example, a person may not notice abuse from an opponent but may be deeply upset if reminded, say, by his children that his voice is unworthy of the latest hit record. Every one has the basic desires this example supports. The actual blend is unique to the individual, but no one is totally without a portion of each. The fundamental desires are:

1   Food and drink
2   Comfort and shelter
3   Freedom from fear and danger
4   Social approval
5   Self-esteem
6   To attract the opposite sex
7   To love and be loved
8   To live longer

This list encompasses all the sources of human emotion. Often these emotions may show in some physiological form, such as sweating, a dry mouth, goosepimples, tears or as tension shown in backache or neckache, toothache or headache, and so on. But the more pleasing aspects come from that part of the personality which makes people likeable. These are positive factors which, although often exploited by sellers, nevertheless bring great benefit and satisfaction to the people concerned.

1   Food and drink
Few people in the advanced countries today really know the effects of hunger or thirst and so their satisfaction has ceased to be recognised as a basic drive. But the experiences of the few driven to cannibalism and the like under extreme conditions are surely an indication of what could be. Besides, it was only a hundred or so years ago that children of 8 or 9 years old risked being hanged for stealing a loaf of bread.

2   Comfort and shelter
Once again, the experience of total deprivation is limited to few, but the many thousands anxious to buy their own homes in the face of prohibitive prices must experience some emotional upheaval, enough to drive them almost to distraction.

3   Freedom from fear and danger
To twentieth-century man, the motor car, smoking, alcohol and over-eating provide the real dangers. However, the incidence of danger appears so remote that the average person does not believe its consequences could happen to him. Certainly a direct confrontation with the possibilities of danger usually proves to be anti-productive. Posters on road accidents and anti-smoking campaigns appear to have been ignored by the majority.

4   Social approval
Many successful marketing campaigns have prospered through customers wishing 'to keep up with the Jones'. The part of built-in obsolescence that promotes the annual face-lift or change of model is a direct appeal to this human need. Caravans and boats are items that seem to owe much of their saleability to the prestige ownership seems to bring.

5   Self-esteem
Each person must have self-respect. To do so they must experience a feeling of superiority. To be able to respect themselves everyone must believe they are a little bit better than the next man, and that

whatever they do is always the result of better thinking or judgment. Everyone thinks this way, and everyone needs to think this way. It is why so many advertisers feature their products in a setting totally untypical of the average purchaser. The average purchaser tends to visualise himself or herself in that setting. Often, of course, they do not *see* the quite considerable differences. People establish a close affinity with the environment of their daydreams – an association of roles and circumstances.

6   To attract the opposite sex
Freud expressed this desire more blatantly, but prudence has changed the basic drive to that of the chase rather than the kill. However, in selling or advertising terms, the principle is a continuing best-seller. Even if Freud was wrong, and that is disputed, in describing it as the strongest desire, in modern marketing terms he could not be more right.

7   To love and to be loved
The theme has been used for a detergent, for frozen peas, tobacco and numerous other products. It appeals largely to the maternal instinct and to young love. The makers of Persil have persevered, and one assumes succeeded, with their theme of maternal love and 'whiteness shows'. Heinz 'Soup Generation' series and Readibrek 'Central Heating for Kids' are continuing winners with universal appeal, projecting family love and togetherness. Others are less certain.

8   To live longer
Judging by the amount spent on health there is no shortage of scope for the seller, provided that the claims made can be substantiated. There are some 'services' that cannot.

These eight desires demand satisfaction. In the past, religion was almost the only solace for the working population. Even today the only real hope of satisfying all these desires seems to lie in self-discipline generated by religious faith. Yet the most rewarding aspects of these desires seem to be the positive ones. Freedom from fear and danger, and the desire to live longer are comparatively weak areas for the salesman to work on. The insurance or assurance salesman must never state the obvious, but if he speaks in positive terms, such as tax benefits, savings potential, security of income and the like, he seems to gain good results. Salesmen win orders by satisfying such needs.

It is by showing the prospect that his real, unspoken needs may be satisfied that many successful salesmen make use of the 'sixth' sense. Not many people admit to understanding how it works, for it is often known as an intuition. In the selling game it involves providing psychological clues which win the unwitting approval of the customer, so establishing an almost telepathic relationship. It is because of this contrived personality trait that good salesmen are described as 'born salesmen'. In fact, it is more likely that successful salesmen tend to come from the highly perceptive members of the community: those that feel mood and sense attitude, and respond accordingly. By so reacting to need they sell themselves to prospects. And when they have won the genuine confidence of another person, then that person rewards them accordingly.

Clearly people who succeed in selling could just as likely have succeeded in the theatre, in politics or as social workers.

The behavioural aspects are considered in more detail in Chapter 12.

Organisation for selling

Now that the mystique of selling has been dispelled, let us consider a more mundane and yet, for the vast majority, a more critical aspect – the organisation of the selling job. In any case, the personality traits already specified are within everyone, for we all practise the principles described in order to mix well and to live our everyday lives. The better salesmen tend to be particularly perceptive, but that is a talent which can be developed with training. However, no salesman succeeds who does not organise himself in his selling job. To be successful he practises the principles of planned selling. This means having a plan of campaign for each customer, knowing exactly what products it will profit the customer to buy and the benefits the salesman can emphasise that will encourage him to buy. Arranged carefully, this approach will enable the salesman to increase the number of orders he will collect. The sales presentation he will have worked out will flow quite naturally once the method is understood. For it enables the salesman to direct and control an interview, knowing at all times the route he is taking through the buyer's mind. Planned selling consists of:

1 Building business
2 Journey planning
3 The sales sequence
4 Personal organisation

Each of these activities is essential to successful selling. As they are the vital means by which the salesman makes his contribution to the firm's prosperity, it is advisable to consider each activity in some detail. Although they will be considered separately, it must be understood that they are interdependent.

1 Building business
The commercial and industrial scene is constantly changing. Firms close down and others start up. Some move away and others move in. A few will change buyers, some favourable and others unfavourable to any one concern. A small proportion will be growing rapidly and a few others will be declining. In a period of five years the total market situation is likely to have changed beyond recognition. So the active salesman will not only be ensuring that lost business is replaced but will also be continually finding and winning new customers.

To build business a few definite disciplines must be followed. First, the salesman must reserve a portion of each working week to the business of opening new accounts. While the better part of this time will be devoted to obtaining relevant information, it should include a fixed amount of time spent with prospects. In addition to providing opportunities for bringing in new business, it will also assist the salesman in maintaining his presentation at a high pitch, for habitual calling on established contacts allows bad practices to develop.

Often the best business-building prospects are contained within a salesman's established customers. A number will buy a limited amount of supplies from a range of suppliers, giving the bulk to one or two trusted firms. The active salesman will prepare for each prospect a detailed specification of needs and buying habits. He wins the confidence of buyers by showing an understanding of their problems and by offering suggestions and ideas. Because of his travels and because of the information fed to him by his employer, he is able to become a focal point of industrial information. By coupling his knowledge and by using his own firm's resources, the salesman is soon able to become the major and the most reliable source of information to buyers. Now, while this does not mean that the buyer will automatically reward the salesman by showering him with orders, it does ensure that the salesman is always seen and this alone increases his face-to-face selling time. He must use that valuable time effectively. The professional salesman sets himself targets for such activity performances.

2 Journey planning

Time is the most valuable commodity of the salesman. He must use it wisely. Sensible buyers appreciate the value of a salesman's time and do not allow it to be wasted. Buyers that place restrictions on time devoted to seeing salesmen are simply not doing their job. Good commercial buyers believe that their most fruitful activity is listening to salesmen. They believe that salesmen bring profit opportunity. Sadly such buyers are rare. In some countries they are almost non-existent. In the UK they too often appear to be company secretaries, office managers or even clerks whose minor function is to see salesmen, collect literature for filing and to make occasional complaints. These people totally disregard the buying function, except at Christmas when they expect to collect their turkey or some such reward. The buying decision in these circumstances may not be in the best interests of the employers. The practice is certainly not in the best interests of the national economy.

The salesman attempts to maximise his selling time by planning his daily journey. This may be aided by gluing a street guide onto hardboard, sticking in coloured map pins to indicate calls and then putting elastic bands – of different colours – around the appropriate daily journey. Through pre-selecting a particular route the salesman learns to economise on time by estimating his arrival at each call and he is therefore able to fix appointments for a number of calls, particularly those at the beginning and the end of the day. Furthermore, he is able to allocate the amount of time he spends with each prospect. Now he is in a position to devote his best time to the best prospects.

As he works out his daily calling programme the salesman sees the advantages in travelling during non-selling time or while buying propensity is at a low peak. He makes his longest journey before the start of the working day so as to arrive at his first call promptly. Any necessary travel during the day will be between the hours 12.00 and 2.00 p.m. This enables him to maximise his face-to-face selling time. Alternatively, that time may be spent in the local library catching up on current events in the locality and, in the reference section, updating customer profiles.

Ideally, the salesman should use a time-planning analysis record, showing a breakdown of the major activities of each day totalled into 'selling time' and 'non-selling time'. By keeping this analysis he is able to carry out improvements in his daily work programme. Besides, the salesman should regard himself as a production machine, with a schedule prepared to furnish orders.

3 The sales sequence

The sales sequence is often confused with a standardised sales presentation. The standardised presentation is a prepared sales talk developed by experienced salesmen. While it has the disadvantage of sounding stilted and artificial when put into the mouths of unknowing new recruits, it does give them a vocabulary and provides them with early confidence in their selling job. Properly understood it will also give the basis for a sound yet flexible presentation after induction and following some applied experience.

The sales sequence is based on the same principles but is developed by the salesman himself with the aid of his field sales manager. In effect it is a work programme for the selling activity based on the capacity of the individual and the needs of his employer. The sales sequence is the essential implementation of the company sales policy. In recent years it has become incorporated in the company sales manual. It is based on:

(*a*) Company sales policy
(*b*) Attitudes to the buyer
(*c*) Company products and services
(*d*) Securing interviews

(*e*) The sales talk
(*f*) The presentation
(*g*) Closing the sale
(*h*) Overcoming objections

In order to understand how the salesman undertakes his selling job it is beneficial to consider the details of the sales sequence more thoroughly.

(*a*) *Company sales policy*. The sales policy is usually contained within the marketing plan and may often be revealed through study of the sales budget. Investigation will reveal the quotas set for the numerous activities of selling, apart from achievement of sales performance in the chosen product mix. Salesmen that simply pursue increased sales turnover are not necessarily choosing the most profitable route. In some firms a £2000 order may bring infinitely more profit than a £20 000 order, even though relative profit margins, say 10%, are the same.

(*b*) *Attitudes to the buyer*. The buyer is not a machine, he is a human being. He trusts people he likes and distrusts those he doesn't like. He makes the best and most rational decision that is possible. But the larger part of any buying decision is one of judgment and so it is emotive. He will pay more for one of two identical products if he believes it to be more reliable, or that the maker will ensure that it is trouble-free. He is prepared to pay extra for freedom from doubt. Like every other buyer, he suffers from cognitive dissonance and he tries to avoid it by paying a premium price. Even if the merits of two competing companies are unknown to the purchaser, he may be prepared to pay more, believing that he is getting better value for money. Moreover, because the prospect is human, he likes to be considered knowledgeable. It is not unusual for the salesman, knowing a new product is about to be launched, to discuss with buyers the needs for a new product, carefully noting the advice of each prospect. If he guides the interview along the right lines he gets at least three constructive suggestions from each buyer, knowing that they are already incorporated in the new product. When the product is launched he visits each prospect in turn, thanking them, on behalf of the company, for their valuable help and showing them the product they have helped to design in accordance with their own expressed needs. Where possible he follows this visit up with a letter of appreciation so that the buyer proudly shows it round. That letter must include details of the specific points made by the buyer. By showing it around the buyer is 'selling' the advantages to his colleagues.

One word of advice. This technique must not be overdone. Furthermore, stressed points made by the buyer and not incorporated in the product must be treated as buying objections and resolved accordingly.

Too often people think that salesmen have to be good talkers. It is true that they have to persuade, but persuasion is best carried out by the individual on himself. Buyers are no exception. So the salesman is essentially a good listener. By asking the right questions he gets the buyer to make his own buying pressure and to overcome his own objections. In doing this he ensures that the interview is devoted entirely to the interests of the buyer – and also, as it happens, to the long-term interests of the seller. It gives the buyer the feeling of importance he needs – a feeling common to all buyers. It is why they seek the job.

(*c*) *Company products and services.* As we have seen, successful marketing depends on satisfying the real needs of the buyer. The buyer does not buy a machine, he buys profit, output or opportunity. He must be sold these benefits. So knowing one's product is not as important as knowing what it will do and what it will not do. Likewise, the seller shows that he knows how his product compares with competitive opportunities.

Furthermore, the salesman studies his company's supporting services. He knows when to offer credit, how the tax system benefits a purchase now, and how maintenance and service contracts, where appropriate, operate. The buyer must never be allowed to find supporting information for himself. The successful salesman has supporting aids in the form of dcf calculations, feature articles from the quality press, a prepared list of questions and answers, reports on the usage by approving customers and a specially written specification suited to the prospect. In his covering letter the salesman refers to particular points raised by the buyer and indicates where explanations may be found. He makes sure that the buyer is given better than full acknowledgment in writing for the part he has played. The professional salesman gets his reward and satisfaction in the form of orders, not by trying to prove to the buyer what a superior salesman he is. Good salesmen never sell, they find buyers shrewd enough to buy from them.

(*d*) *Securing interviews.* In general, more calls mean more selling time. And that means more orders. Now this does not mean that the salesman must devote himself to maximising his call rate at the expense of all other considerations. It means that he should conduct an interview with an objective in mind, secure that objective and depart. More time spent in preparing for a call results in less wasted time during the call. This is the first step in ensuring an interview. The salesman with an objective in mind has a worthwhile reason for calling. It is not merely another contact visit. The buyer soon learns that his caller is always worth seeing – he will always get something of value from him.

Once in the presence of the buyer it is essential to win his instant attention. If the salesman fails to win the buyer's interest within the first twenty seconds, his success barometer falls drastically. So he gives the buyer something to do. The buyer is given something to hold – something to look at or feel, to taste or smell. He is not talked at because his mind is still full of his immediately previous activity. That spell must be broken. In the absence of all other inspiration, a copy of the local paper thrust into his hand followed by a question on the lead item will often do.

The objective at the interview must never be to secure an order. Salesmen make customers. The objective is to satisfy the buyer's need with a product beneficial to him. The interview must be devoted to that objective, and prepared and undertaken accordingly. The opening remarks always refer directly to the problems associated with the need. By highlighting the need the buyer is attuned to the direction of the interview. He is made to realise that the salesman understands his problems and is willing to be a helpful ally in their solution. All human characteristics prevail in the animal kingdom. Often points of human failings or strengths are illustrated by reference to a particular animal. Now we have much to learn from dogs. Dogs are man's best friend because they will always greet him with enthusiasm and excitement. A tail may even seem to be wagging the whole body. Taking a hint, the salesman will always try to show his delight at seeing the buyer. He may do this with the warmth of his greeting or he may use the magic of a smile – few people feel that they can resist a smile given freely and without inhibition. Smiles make a person look more presentable and they engender friendliness in the meeting.

Each interview is therefore the preparation for the next. Securing the first interview may be difficult, but with a definite objective and something relevant to say an approach by letter or telephone can prepare the ground. When suggesting an appointment the salesman gives the buyer two alternatives to choose from, by time and by day. He does not leave him with the choice he may adopt himself – a yes or a no.

(*e*)   *The sales talk.* All sales points need to be credible. The seller contrives to provide supporting evidence. He uses his voice as a persuasive instrument: variations in tone and pace, liberal uses of pauses, supported by the hands for explanation – either by gesture or by writing down a point for the buyer to see as well as hear – are all necessary. The use of words is important. The salesman chooses active verbs – at least 50% of all verb forms used should be active. Moreover, half of all nouns used should be concrete. Adjectives and adverbs should only be used when they are needed for precision. Where they are used to express opinion, then that is made quite clear to the prospect otherwise there are dangers arising under the Trades Descriptions Act. Prepositions are always to be preferred to prepositional phrases. Meanwhile, the salesman who succeeds takes great care to perfect his diction and English usage. Often he will rehearse his presentation on tape and amend the unsuitable – and he may even rehearse in front of a mirror so that he can vet the image he is projecting.

(*f*)   *The sales presentation.* These are the golden minutes of selling. It is where all the preparation counts. The major selling points appealing to the motives of the particular buyer are supported by visual aids or by a demonstration. At each step the seller tries to get the agreement of the buyer to the point being made. At the finish of the presentation the salesman repeats the selling points that appeared to attract the prospect the most. All the time looking for buying signals, he probes for the real, perhaps hidden, reason behind the more active interest shown by the buyer.

(*g*)   *Closing the sale.* Because they fear rejection, many people fail as salesmen, simply because they will not ask for the order. The best salesmen try to judge the point at which the opportunity for agreement is best and then suggest some alternatives for the buyer to choose. They do not give him the chance to say yes or no; rather they suggest black or white, 100 or 200, delivered next week or next month.

Thus the seller encourages the buyer to make a choice between one of two favourable alternatives.

(*h*) *Overcoming objections.* Properly prepared, the sales presentation will overcome objections before they arise. But some strategy is necessary. Buyers like to buy. They do not like being sold. Now if the salesman presents a faultless case, the buyer will create an objection so that he can be seen to be performing his buying job. He also needs some time to grasp the essentials and he will find this time by raising an objection with no real foundation. In other words, he will raise objections that cannot be overcome because they are purely fictitious. We all do this. We see something we like, but we have to consider every alternative before returning and deciding on the preferred purchase. Experienced salesmen know this characteristic and leave minor faults in their presentation so that the buyer can spot them and feel he is doing his job. Because they are minor faults and because they are deliberate, they may easily be overcome. Honour is satisfied.

4 Personal organisation

Organisation can be the essence of good selling. The personal organisation of the salesman, who is away from an office, a secretary and a convenient telephone for much of the time, is critical. Apart from planning his time he must constantly be analysing the market and finding prospects. He must keep adequate records of customers, their transactions and dealings, and their potential, together with relevant industrial information. Furthermore, he must write informative sales reports such that the content is as valuable to him as it is to his management.

Successful selling is one of the most rewarding careers open to man. It provides him with untold opportunities. But the greatest danger to beware of is being recognised as a 'good' salesman. If he looks like a salesman, sounds like a salesman and behaves like a salesman, he will fail because he cannot be a salesman.

10

Selling and Sales Management

Selling has been shown as the most dynamic element in the business environment. Yet despite the disciplines inherent in the planned selling method, salesmen need directions. It is not that they, as a breed, are unable to decide their own priorities but that each sales territory is only one part of a larger and wider selling operation. Although the individual salesman may well be competent to judge the changing market situation locally, it is unlikely that he will have the time and the skills necessary to *anticipate* these changes. Furthermore, whatever the local situation and its changing demand scales, the salesman must sell the product mix most profitable to his company. So although he, in isolation, may find that he is able to sell a different mix more easily, he must either adjust his activities to meet company needs or advise management of the possibilities on his territory. From this advice the company may find it expedient to substitute some parts of his quota with those of a salesman in another territory with a similar problem. In this way one may compensate for another. By coordinating the activities of the members of the sales force in this way, the sales manager performs one of his most critical operational tasks.

The job of sales manager is analysing the market, recommending selling strategy and then recruiting the sales force needed to achieve pre-set sales goals. He is responsible for control of the selling effort.

Before considering the job of the sales manager in some detail, it may be advisable to relate the sales manager's position to that of the marketing manager. Essentially, the present-day job of the sales manager is no different from that which he has always practised. But there was a transitional period during the emergence of mass advertising, market research and information management when the sales manager's role changed. He became responsible for these support-to-selling activities and became the marketing manager. Because of the changing emphasis it was thought in some circles that the role of the salesman was finished. Management attempted to substitute the salesman role, easily the most expensive market communication activity with supporting activities. But it soon recognised that the salesman was still the most effective seller of goods and services, even if the most expensive. Once this was recognised, sales managers were appointed to make the best possible use of this costly asset. The job of sales management, then, is the deployment of this asset in the most profitable manner.

In some companies the marketing manager reports to the sales director. This apparent anomaly arose in companies where the sales manager's job remained pre-eminent but where marketing services, including publicity, research and planning, had been put in the hands of a newly appointed marketing manager. In these companies there was never any doubt about the value of the salesman.

The job of sales management

For convenience the sales manager's job may be divided into the following categories:

1 Planning
2 Organisation
3 Recruitment and selection
4 Training
5 Running sales meetings
6 Motivating
7 Directing
8 Monitoring
9 Harmonising
10 Field sales supervision

It is clear from this list that the real job of the sales leader is management. Man management is the central theme of any sales leader's task. Historically, skills in management were considered a natural in-born talent, a flair which somehow coincided with intelligence. This view has now been largely discarded. Knowledge of management is acquired in much the same way as knowledge of engineering or accounting. The relationship between knowledge and ability is not, however, so close as it is in the natural sciences. Despite their own considerable knowledge of management techniques, people still fail. Moreover, people without such knowledge sometimes succeed. What does seem clear is that there is a better chance of success with knowledge than there could be without it. The sales manager is no different from any other functional manager; he needs to practise skills developed from a realistic body of knowledge built up over many years by men of experience. The sales manager uses this acquired knowledge to perform his job.

1   Planning the selling effort

The first priority of the sales manager is in the planning of his own time. He must first establish his priorities, allocate time to the various tasks, develop a workable schedule and delegate the minor functions he cannot handle personally. By following this procedure he stands some chance of fulfilling his programme. In sales management all crises seem to arise at the same time and all targets likewise come into sight together. If time is not rationed and priorities predetermined, the sales manager could easily sink beneath the flood of calls on his time.

But this policy will work only if his overall planning procedures are within his capability to control. The elements within his span of influence are:

(*a*)   The salesmen
(*b*)   The sales territories
(*c*)   The customers
(*d*)   The products

As the emphasis here is on planning, it is the future trends that matter, and these are subject to the continuing influence of the sales manager. His plans for each of these performance determinants need separate consideration.

(a)   The salesmen
Salesmen have always been judged by performance. They grew up

with payment by results, principally because of commission on sales schemes. Although the measure of performance principle has not changed much, salesmen today enjoy a measure of security through combined salaries and incentives.

It is perfectly equitable to measure salesmen by their performance, one against the other, provided that their opportunities are equal. In actual practice, however, they do not enjoy such equal opportunities. Unfortunately, it is almost impossible for the individual company to measure market sales potential in sufficient detail and with the necessary accuracy. It is also impractical to constantly change territorial boundaries because potential has changed. So management needs some other means of comparing and measuring *selling* performance as opposed to *sales* performance. The most appropriate method is to decide the activities necessary to perform the selling job, to apply weighting factors and then to establish quotas accordingly. These activities include the number of calls, selling costs/enquiries, cost per call, average value of orders, canvassing calls, number of orders obtained, etc. (See John Stapleton, *How to Prepare a Marketing Plan*, The Gower Press, 1982.) By establishing clear programmes of activities for salesmen and by working out conversion ratios for every activity, the sales manager is providing the basis for his future selling efforts. He is therefore planning the activities of the salesman.

(b)   The sales territories

It has already been said that calculating market sales potential by territory is really beyond the scope of the ordinary small-to-medium firm. Notwithstanding this point, it is still necessary for the company to estimate at least the present market size, the company share, and industry and company growth prospects alike. But even this data is unlikely to be as helpful as a sales analysis showing company achievement on each territory, preferably by product, by size, by class of outlet and, where possible, by direct marketing costs. Moreover, information as to gross profit earned by territory and the number of dormant accounts when compared with the national average should indicate the likely areas of attack. These will then be included in the plan of campaign devised to support the field salesman.

Where possible, each sales territory is built up from distinct regions for which separate statistics are available. These may be by county, by Registrar-General's regions or by television areas. By conforming to these boundaries it is possible for a company to make use of published statistics in planning for growth. In the absence of other factual information it is possible to calculate national averages per head of population and to use these figures as a determinant for market size. Provided that the sales manager realises that the figures he is using are no more than indicative, he may find them significant in planning terms. For example, if sales penetration on a territory is far beneath the national average, then reasons may be sought. Investigation often reveals a clue to improved sales. In practice sales managers may allocate sales territories according to number of outlets. Although useful, it does not allow for growth potential, nor for really significant accounts justifying additional attention.

(c) The customers
As we have already shown, customers' operating performances do not always move in a uniform pattern. Their suppliers, in their own interests, need to identify the growth opportunities confronting customers and then to concentrate their energies on supplying those that seize these opportunities. To grow is to serve growth markets.

Sometimes a company may have to select customers with the necessary potential and then guide them towards opportunities. Whichever applies, the companies concerned must be selected from among the many. Some will be very small, others may be large. Between the two extremes will be concerns capable of buying a successful small competitor and so improving their own potential. Sales management is the function that controls the activities necessary to bring orders today and reports to top management on the opportunities *in the market place* tomorrow.

To carry out this analysis all customers and potential customers are grouped according to size by SIC (Standard Industrial Classification). Changes between groups are soon spotted and causes investigated. Furthermore, where a company has a diverse product range it will subdivide the analysis into product groups. This may appear a mammoth task, but it is probably already extracted in those companies most likely to adopt the system in its preparation of the sales forecast. In really large companies it is no more than a print-out from the computer, while small companies, on the other hand, will not have so many accounts to investigate.

Marketing-orientated companies are those that consider the implications on customers of every critical business decision. So monitoring the performance of these customers is just as necessary a part of the marketing frame as it is an essential control device for sales management. Besides which, the information needed by sales management on customers will be contained within the customer profile records kept by the salesmen in order to perform their everyday selling task. Such is the desirable structure of marketing information systems – entirely modular in nature.

(d)   The products

The sales manager influences product policy and product development, because he alone is able to advise on the continuing conflict between volume and price from purely market conditions. He may not have the skills to equate supply and demand quantitatively, but because of his communicating role between customer and management he is able to provide the necessary qualitative appraisal. This subjective approach is critical because sales returns do not arrive by discrete units as shown on a demand curve, they arrive by customer order. Moreover, orders are not of equal value, nor do they have a 'normal distribution' among customers. Price increases hit the biggest buyers hardest. They also find it easy to secure alternative sources. And they will, if their assessment of service supplied shows a negative differential to the likely price difference. Mathematics will not identify this possibility – the sales manager should. The price elasticity of demand remains his province. In this position he provides guidance on product policy decisions and tends to represent the interests of his customers when such discussions take place. Planning the selling effort is an essential part of the marketing plan. The benefits of the effort are derived from the disciplines involved in producing the plan, looking for answers and preparing solutions.

2   Organisation of the selling effort

The sales organisation is created and maintained in order to achieve the company's 'rolling' objectives. There is no one best type of sales organisation and the different types each have their merits. The choice of a particular organisation will have depended partly upon the circumstances facing the company and largely on the resources available.

Sales organisations have gone through some change during the past twenty years. Clearly this transition has been parallel to the changes in the patterns of distribution. Selling to a new distribution channel demands a different selling organisation. Often the change is made in order to ensure control over the firm's actual selling effort, rather than leaving it to a distributor of some kind. Avon established its own network of sales girls in order to short-circuit the restrictions inherent in the franchise system prevailing in the cosmetic industry. Tupperware brought its party-plan selling ideas to the UK and was quickly matched by Sarah Coventry and Pippa-dee. Pyramid selling won many early recruits but quickly became discredited. Other changes in the organisation of selling effort involved the use of revitalised promotional devices and aids, and the reduction of personal sales contribution; mail order, vending machines and self-service are prime examples. These changes were prompted by the costs of sales personnel, the need for superior and more leisurely presentation, and the advent of volume sales. They are more easily subjected to a routine selling procedure, with less versatility required at the point of purchase.

However, four considerations are essential in the organisation of a sales force:

(*a*) The need to serve the customer
(*b*) The duties and procedures involved in serving the customer
(*c*) The personalities required to serve the customer
(*d*) The degree of responsibility and authority necessary to make decisions regarding the customer.

All decisions affecting the sales organisation must be taken in full consideration of the present and ultimate effect upon the customer. The choice between agents or distributors as an alternative to salesmen will be taken according to the needs imposed on the manufacturer by his customers, for the sales organisation is provided to serve the customer and is an essential part of the 'added value' he expects in the price he pays. The actual types of selling organisation prevailing conform to these criteria. Each type involves a different *degree* of selling, combined with a required supporting qualification. In practice many firms recruit a technically qualified man in the belief that he will sell better because he is technically compatible with both the customer and the products. The argument of this being a better alternative to the experienced salesman being taught sufficient technical knowledge is invalid. Both succeed as well as fail.

These selling jobs are:

(*a*) Speciality selling
(*b*) Pioneer (or commando) selling
(*c*) Industrial selling
(*d*) Consumer durables selling
(*e*) Consultant engineers
(*f*) Missionary (or propaganda) selling
(*g*) Repeat consumer selling
(*h*) Retail selling
(*i*) Merchandising

Not all these need amplification. Speciality selling is practised generally where there is a once-only selling opportunity, or at least where there is little likelihood of a repeat sale in the near future. It is a selling job which requires the salesman to assess a need and sell his line all at the same interview, usually from cold. Reward is largely by commission, and because of the pressures involved turnover of personnel is high. The system includes assurance salesmen, some office equipment salesmen and those selling advertising space, although this category is fast moving away from the speciality field, the exception being in the sale of some directories and annuals.

Missionary or propaganda selling is almost unique to pharmaceutical products. Salesmen call and 'sell' to doctors who do not buy but specify to chemists who do not consume but supply to patients who have no choice. Other selling jobs are easily identifiable to the non-marketing executive. What is common to them all, however, is the tendency to reject the salesmanship aspect of the job by emphasising the 'representative' expression. This is but a sop to the salesmen: everyone knows what his job is – it is he and his management who try to pretend it is something different. This may be for good reasons, but it is still unnecessary.

3   Recruitment and selection

The sales manager of today has considerable help in recruitment. He may have a personnel department or he may use a selection consultant. Recruitment presents few horrors to the sales manager, unless it be the sheer volume of applications he is bound to receive. Selection, however, is the real problem. As no one has resolved the problem of what makes salesmen succeed and, if they do, why they cannot repeat their performance in another company or another industry, the sales manager's task is unenviable. He must use his judgment. Provided that he has analysed the selling job adequately and prepared a realistic job description, and then used this in conjunction with merit-rating reports of his best men to produce a man profile – a description of the type of man most likely to succeed in the job – he has improved his chances of success immensely. But no more than that.

Some of the most commonly specified characteristics are:

(*a*)   To be perceptive of people's attitudes and needs
(*b*)   To have ambition, motivation and be a self-starter
(*c*)   To indicate presentation, health and poise
(*d*)   To show business sense, curiosity and mental abilities
(*e*)   To suggest courtesy, friendliness and persuasiveness
(*f*)   To generate creativeness, knowledge and originality
(*g*)   To provide enthusiasm, flexibility and integrity
(*h*)   To have figure sense and good handwriting and speech
(*i*)   To evince loyalty and self-control

A person who has all these talents would not necessarily make a good salesman, but they are typical, in part, of the most desirable characteristics. In the selection process it is not unusual for the salesman to be put in the hot seat. It is a position he will occupy often enough when confronted by customers.

4   Training the salesman

Salesmen spend most of their time without direct supervision. They are continuously going through the same routine, numerous times each day, of presenting their products, and emphasising and re-emphasising the benefits of particular products. In return, they hear every day all the reasons why most prospects do not buy from their company. Some of the remarks may be derogatory, others may simply state why their existing suppliers are superior. Under such constant pressure it is not surprising that an individual salesman becomes disorientated. Training is intended to provide a satisfactory balance to the problem. Furthermore, during the course of his journeys the salesman is constantly mixing with the salesmen of other companies and industries. He will tend to adopt the general characteristics of these people unless his employer takes the trouble to give him training in attitudes, work habits and procedures. Salesmen are good at their jobs because of their chameleon-like personalities, changing to every mood and responding to every whim of the customer. If they are not given regular training and reorientation they soon become biased in favour of their customers.

The better form of training will usually consist of a combination of theoretical instruction and practice in the classroom and practical training on the job. Training for new recruits or retraining for established salesmen will normally consist of:

(*a*) *Background knowledge:* the company, its history and organisation; procedures and routines; policy; long-term plans; promotion policies. The industry, formation, structure, market shares, competition.

(*b*) *Work planning and organisation:* journey cycles, selective selling, customer records, information seeking, prospecting for business.

(*c*) *Sales techniques:* customer needs, preparation of material, obtaining interviews, sales presentation, sound talking techniques, overcoming objections, closing, selling after-sales service.

(*d*) *Supporting the selling effort:* product knowledge, reporting procedures, administration, entertaining, merchandising, personal promotion, car driving.

By providing a training programme the sales manager is obliged to analyse the selling job and to develop standards of performance. This makes it possible for the salesman himself to spot his own deficiencies and remedy them before they become apparent to his colleagues. Eventually a training programme will bring sufficient discipline and guidance to help avoid major deficiencies arising at all.

5 Sales meetings

The sales meeting is used as a vital training activity. The more preparation the sales manager puts into the meeting, the greater the results. In establishing his sales meetings' programme through the year, he starts off with a clear objective and makes sure that the reason behind each meeting is clearly defined. Consistent with clear-cut objectives is the adoption of a theme for each meeting, each theme conforming to some part of marketing strategy. Having adopted real commercial reasons for running the sales meetings, the sales manager uses some form of monitoring device to enable him to seek and find improvements.

Meetings are beneficial to the salesmen and the company alike because they help to consolidate the link between management and the sales force. This often eases the stress on communications. By providing a forum the sales manager gives an opportunity to those within the company to mix and discuss common problems. Moreover, the gathering together of the men fosters a sense of belonging and reminds them of the vital contribution each makes to the company's well-being. In addition, the sales meeting is the ideal occasion to explain new policies, company plans, projects and developments, and the members of the sale force are able to contribute and exchange information about new ideas, notable achievements and sales tactics. In this way the sales manager reinforces his training programme. The alternative themes open to the sales manager may include:

(a) Achieving the forecasted product mix
(b) Opening and developing new markets
(c) Prospecting for new business
(d) Using sales promotional material
(e) Record-keeping
(f) Selling the after-sales service
(g) Converting inquiries to orders
(h) Selling expense cost ratios

These are no more than indicative of the range of subjects the sales manager may use. Ideally, the year's programme will be built up from an analysis of selling problems recorded in the annual marketing plan.

The sales meeting is the platform upon which the sales manager gains or enhances the respect of the members of his team. Even well-known public speakers have some trepidation before speaking. This may show at the start. However, once into his subject, the sales manager should soon interest his men in what he has to say, for he should be close enough to them to speak their language. To ensure that he makes the most effective impact he attempts to:

(*a*)   Highlight the most relevant points
(*b*)   Emphasise the importance of the subject
(*c*)   Use visual aids
(*d*)   Start with a practical example
(*e*)   Make his own enthusiasm contagious

Because he realises he is making a sales presentation to his men he adopts the techniques involved in a proper buyer/seller interview. He ensures that every step follows a logical sequence and is qualified by examples and illustrations sufficient to register with the audience. He uses pauses to let points sink in. He does not use too much detail, for that may be contained in handouts, and instead concentrates on making principles clear, for they are most likely to be remembered. And to reinforce his presentation he summarises his major points, so shaping the talk as a whole in the minds of his listeners.

6 Motivating

There are two kinds of motivation: financial and non-financial incentives. Because of the unique nature of their employment salesmen are particularly sensitive to both types of incentive. They know that a little extra effort on their part may bring huge rewards to their company. So by having a payment-by-results scheme the company encourages its salesmen to greater effort by allowing them to share in the benefits they bring. So although money may not be the most important motivator, it is certainly the most powerful and may often be a substitute for the really important incentive. For like his customers, the salesman is subject to the iceberg principle and needs satisfaction for all his eight basic desires.

Yet financial incentives do work for many, and in others they may act as a substitute for satisfaction of real needs. Salesmen operating on salary only tend to recognise the value of the technical support service they provide and get on well with their customers; sometimes it is often difficult to determine exactly where their loyalties lie – with the customer or with their employer. The major advantage from the employer's view is that the salaried salesman is more easy to control than a commissioned man. Commission-only salesmen work solely for financial reward. They tend to concentrate on getting orders and often minimise attention to supporting services since, for them, they take up valuable selling time. Because they are paid on commission alone they may easily work for more than one employer and so devote their time to the more lucrative areas of their territory, making no real attempt to develop their patch.

The salaried man is a cost to the employer irrespective of sales revenue, while the commission-only man is paid out of revenue and bears the risk of the enterprise. Most firms today attempt to compromise between the two extremes and provide a combination of salary and commission; where commission is not easy to evaluate because of a team selling effort, a bonus to salary is provided.

The typical salesman, however, reacts positively to some form of non-financial incentives, simply because the nature of his job makes him seek solace of a more emotional kind. Normally these non-financial incentives consist of:

(*a*) Recognition and appreciation
(*b*) A feeling of belonging
(*c*) A personal challenge
(*d*) Good working conditions
(*e*) Leadership
(*f*) Security

Although these are all straightforward, each one has special connotations for the salesman.

(a) Recognition and appreciation
The job of selling is a simulation for the winning of approval. Salesmen are continually struggling to satisfy their need for accept-

ance. Much of this need can be satisfied by the process of winning orders. However, in the selling job today, a new customer will often place further orders direct as goods are required. This robs the salesman of his regular 'shot'. So a form of compensation is provided by the sales manager during the time he spends with salesmen in the field.

(b) A feeling of belonging
Because of the time spent away from home, with many lonely nights spent in hotel bedrooms, and the isolation away from his colleagues, the salesman may develop lone wolf symptoms. This is dangerous. Selling demands a gregarious animal, so the sales manager attempts to provide a 'feeling of belonging' to the sales force. He often does this by sending them information, by asking their advice and through newsletters keeping them in touch.

(c) A personal challenge
Setting targets or quotas gives a man something to aim at. By giving him goals the sales manager is removing uncertainty and inviting cooperation.

(d) Good working conditions
To the salesman this means a respectable car, reasonable travel and accommodation expenses, and a system of working that he can easily follow.

(e) Leadership
Everyone needs to feel that there is someone to whom they can turn in times of stress: someone in whom they have confidence and who is capable of inspiring them to greater effort when circumstances warrant it.

(f) Security
It is a fallacy that good salesman reject security. What they do reject is the limitations to immediate reward that come with secure jobs. Salesmen usually come from a breed that equates reward with effort, and in order to enjoy the opportunities this may bring they are prepared to accept some of the risks. Salesmen do not differ from any other person in the need for security. But they are more

willing to absorb some of the wider variations in their fortunes, to rely more on their own skills rather than sink them into a general pool, and to take their chances accordingly. Their need for security shows in their efforts to succeed.

7 Directing the sales effort

In Chapter 9 the need for a time-planning analysis for salesmen was stressed. Earlier in this chapter it was shown that the sales manager needs to plan his time effectively. The emphasis on time is not unrealistic. Out of a 365-day year the salesman averages 250 working days after weekends and holidays have been deducted. If he makes his first call at 8.30 a.m. and his last at about 5.30 p.m. he has managed an 8-hour day, of which about two-thirds may have been spent in travelling, parking and waiting to see the buyer. He needs to be kept waiting only an average of 10 minutes per call for as few as six calls a day to have wasted an hour. Parking may take a similar amount of time. So the salesman has a productivity problem. He needs to maximise his time. The sales manager in helping his men to overcome time problems by, say, saving each man one hour per day, will have increased their total available time by 12½% and their actual selling time by a staggering 40% to 50%.

Similarly, salesmen do not always recognise the value of their time. Study of records often reveals that a salesman will call six times a year on accounts placing orders twice a year with values between £20 and £100. Working out the cost of a salesman's selling time at, say, 3 hours a day 250 days a year equals 750 available selling hours. Taking the cost of the salesman on the road plus his car at £25 000 per year, we can see that his selling time costs £33·33 per hour. There is clearly no profit in such calls, particularly when one considers that the supporting services behind the salesman, all linked directly to his returns, may cost as much again or more than his own direct selling costs. The sales manager shows him how to make the most effective use of his selling time. He helps him to divide his accounts into categories, showing the vital calls, the desirable calls and the low-priority calls. From these he is expected to select the best 100 prospects – 100 because normally a salesman will be unable adequately to serve more unless his job entails little selling and much straightforward order-taking. There are, of course, extremes: a computer salesman may work on six prospects while the milkman will serve 400 or more.

To help his men become more productive the sales manager sets quotas for their activities as well as their performance, and:

(a) Helps them to prepare their journey plans
(b) Guides them on calling times
(c) Encourages them to make prior appointments
(d) Shows them how to prepare presentations
(e) Cooperates with selective selling
(f) Urges them to ask for an order at any call

8 Monitoring the sales effort

This exercise is best performed in the form of a merit-rating guide. This should be completed in the presence of the salesman, making him understand the reasoning behind every observation recorded. It is essential that the salesman understands that the system is used solely for his benefit. When introducing such a system it has proved prudent to let the salesman retain the merit-rating sheet and then ask him to produce it subsequently at a later date for comparison. A merit-rating form may contain:

(a) Personal qualities
(b) Job knowledge
(c) Personal organisation
(d) Salesmanship

The qualities detailed under each headings are normally contained in the job specification and the related man profile.

At the same time the sales manager is compiling his own records on his salesmen. This form of measurement will be an evaluation of each salesman's activities and how he performs against the national average, most of this information being obtained from daily report of call sheets. At least once a month the sales manager will write to a salesman drawing his attention to some point on the call sheet. He would do this even if he has had no time to study all those submitted. Salesmen conclude that all are being studied.

9 Harmonising the sales effort

Sales territories do not divide nicely into convenient segments. Some substantial users buy centrally through the head office. Who gets the credit? It is the sales manager's job to ensure that such happenings are equitably resolved.

10 Field sales supervision

Field sales supervisors have been used in recent years to carry out that part of the sales manager's job that he finds most time-consuming yet is most vital in the performance of his job, even if his management colleagues do occasionally feel that a reply to their memo about the carpet in a branch office is more important.

Field sales managers are used to bring about sales expansion. As we have already seen, the salesmen's selling time is critical. It is the job of the field sales manager to make that selling time truly productive. He does this by implementing, in detail, the policies outlined in this and the previous chapter. He takes responsibility for planning, training, leading, motivating, directing and controlling the selling effort. He helps the salesmen to create customers, and customer satisfaction and goodwill.

11

Customer Service

Customer service is the last great frontier of marketing management. It has been the least glamorous area because it is not involved directly, or so it is thought, with the customer. So almost by definition it has escaped the attention of the marketing pundits. Yet customer service has probably produced, as a department, more members of top management than any other department. The 'office', as it has long been called, is the nerve centre of a business and, because of the range of services provided, enables anyone with the appropriate ambition to learn, with panoramic vision, the intricacies involved in all operational departments and, more importantly, how they interact with each other.

Although other activities of marketing still show signs of a rapid move towards improvements in productivity, little is heard of how customer service may be improved. Yet the customer service department is an essential aid to those other elements. Really significant improvements in total cannot be achieved without a commensurate reformation in the interacting function. Salesmen cannot develop their selling activities without the office absorbing routine tasks. Distribution cannot be improved without more effective stock control. Advertising will not bring real rewards unless enquiry handling is sharpened. Nor will growth be achieved without adequate attention being given to the major areas of customer service. It is giving attention to all these areas that results in the 'Total Marketing Concept'. Areas of customer service are:

1   Company service strategy
2   Credit control, allowances, returns, discounts, cancellations

3   Hire purchase, credit sales, leasing, factoring, franchising
4   After-sales service; installation, maintenance service, spare parts
5   Customer guarantees and legal controls
6   Stock control
7   Telephone selling
8   Premiums, joint ventures
9   The sales office organisation
10   Enquiry handling
11   The sales supporting service
12   Management information, accounting, computers, operational research

All these elements are designed to be customer-oriented, although they could easily be mistaken for defensive or counter-offensive operational ploys. A few companies have shown how management can use these activities as positive aids to growth. They are worth considering in some detail.

1   Company service strategy

Too often companies dissipate their effort by trying to do too much and are therefore unable to do anything well. The truly efficient companies avoid the temptation to seize every little work opportunity that comes their way. They concentrate on doing what they do well and work hard at it. But what companies can do well is subject to considerable variety. However, the range can be grouped into six categories:

(a)   Full customer service
Here the company tries to cater for a group of customers' every needs. The nearest one can get to this ideal is the mail order house that tries to offer a department store on display in every home.

(b)   Limited product line specialist
This type of company produces basically one product and sells it primarily to one market. This is usually the function of the small firm, but it does happen in some big concerns such as breweries and aircraft manufacturers.

(c) Specific product specialist

In this example the company has one general-purpose product and markets it according to any preselected opportunity. Newspapers and magazines are good examples. Self-adhesive tape or lettering stencils are recent developments, while papermakers are perhaps the best example.

(d) Market specialist

The company chooses a particular market and then tries to provide a comprehensive service. ASDA promotes its one-stop shopping for chosen geographical areas and offers a highly comprehensive range of goods for the family.

(e) 'Specials' producers

Usually this company has some general-purpose machine that is capable of producing custom-specified goods. This is the province of the general engineering company, the jobbing printer or the plastics moulder.

(f) Product line specialist

Often these companies are suppliers of essential services, and in the UK they have mostly been nationalised. They include coal, gas, electricity, railways, postal and telephone services. If not wholly nationalised, they are usually involved in government-supported industries, such as oceanography or rocketry.

These are all strategic in nature but are in essence the first effort at marketing orientation. By implication they each dominate customer service – they are, in fact, customer-orientated, although the product dominates the strategy in more than one example. Yet even where the product must dominate the company, it is clear that customers are identified, clear benefits to them established and the product sold accordingly. In each case the supplier has aided its customers in the development of their markets.

2 Credit control, allowances, returns, discounts, cancellations

This is an area that more often than not is the centre of disruption between a company and its supplier. Clearly this must be avoided.

But more than that it is a source of promotion. Each of the activities listed involves a contact, and with that contact an exchange of documents or correspondence. Moreover, each of these contacts means the transfer of money or credit. Whichever way the money moves there is scope for building goodwill. Clerks trained in customer service see each of these transactions as an opportunity to show courtesy, interest, consideration and efficiency. They are taught to write letters bursting with goodwill and co-operation, and they learn telephone techniques that reflect the image of a well-run personalised company.

This practice is adopted because it is good for the firm both internally and externally. It is good for the firm internally because it breeds morale and good externally because the executives who handle money matters are often the customer's senior management. But even these virtues will be of little avail if the company policy on these executives is too restrictive or, as frequently happens, is so indeterminate that a conscientious but unknowing middle manager implements traditional rulings that bear little relationship to today's needs. For example, one company in Scotland stopped buying from one source because the supplier would not accept the return on its own van of charged packages. The ruling had been made when crates were not charged and were delivered by rail. A valuable relationship was lost because no one thought of customer service whenever circumstances changed.

Suppliers will always receive complaints. If a company finds that it is satisfying everyone all the time, then the chances are that it is cheating itself in some way. It is probably giving too much away. As firms find that another concern is always capable of meeting their demands, then they tend to allow these demands to grow – not necessarily intentionally. It happens because pressures from all round force them to exploit the willing. When they are suddenly let down they blame the other party, not themselves. They make a complaint. It is at this moment that the opportunist supplier acts. He uses the handling of the complaint as a means to build goodwill. Normally the irate customer is well aware that he is being unreasonable, particularly if he has been allowed to let off steam. Properly handled, the complaint can be a major business builder. Some years ago in the essential oil business a buyer was always too busy to see a supplier's salesman. Purchases were small but steady. The salesman had a new line which he was confident the customer would buy in some volume – if only he could get in to see him. On receipt of a small order for an essence, the salesman collected the goods and carried them about in his car until the customer complained. Within three hours of the complaint – the timing was predictable because deliveries were made every fourteen days – the salesman was in the office of the buyer delivering the goods personally and collecting the planned order on the way out. The buyer did not ask why the goods had not been delivered as usual, he was too delighted at having his problem solved by this 'service-orientated' supplier.

3 Hire purchase, credit sales, leasing, factoring, franchising

As before, this aspect of customer service is involved with the movement of money, so all the remarks made earlier apply.

The impact that hire-purchase and credit-sale agreements have had on business is well documented. Frequently suppliers discover that by allowing terms they become part of the banking business. This has allowed them to increase their profit returns quite substantially – not because of exploitation but because it has enabled more people to buy; and it has also meant higher productivity of resources both because of the increase in volume and through earning a profit as a manufacturer and as a banker from the same transaction. Credit cards, cheque cards and money shops and their growing acceptance indicate an increasing move away from cash transactions. Firms are preparing for the day when all business is transacted on credit. Having the immediate use of a purchase negates the cost of the credit, particularly in days of continuing inflation.

Capital equipment firms have already marketed the advantages of leasing equipment. In effect the customers are sharing the costs of expertise involved in the running of the service. Whether it be a computer in industry or a television set in the home, the costs incurred are known and therefore predictable in the future. It is a form of insurance whereby the customer indemnifies himself against unusual occurrences. He buys a trouble-free service.

It has been estimated that well over 10% of the world's trade is now factored. The system may seem reminiscent of feudalism and of bartering on a huge scale, but it has won acceptance and is growing.

Furthermore, it shows every sign of expansion as the world currency crisis develops. Firms anxious to grow in international markets are beginning to obtain comprehensive information sources on international trade to support their own selling efforts.

Franchising is rightly regarded as a channel of distribution. It is also a financial arrangement for the granting of a commercial privilege. It is not new – kings and rulers have granted franchises for centuries, and a 'by appointment' is a franchise to the depicted monarch.

Most petrol stations and British public houses operate on a franchise provided by their suppliers. Perhaps the most notable franchise company of all is Coca-Cola, with business widely established throughout the world.

The major argument in favour of the franchise movement is the opportunity it creates for anyone to become his own boss. It is often cited as the new era of entrepreneurial activity. Quite clearly the system does allow a person to run his own business, at the same time enabling him to enjoy the advantages of belonging to a large corporation. For example, there are cafes and restaurants in most towns, but their quality of service and their prices cover a wide range. A Wimpy Bar, despite being privately owned, has a consistency of facilities, menu, quality and prices. Few people today need to study the menu outside before venturing in; they know the level for which the outlet provides.

Franchising has earned a bad reputation because some franchisers dished out franchises indiscriminately, taking the franchisee's investment and then allowing him to sink without help. Meanwhile, other franchisers, using pyramid selling, built up big distributive organisations through recruitment incentives which made it unnecessary to carry out the distribution of goods except by selling them as stock-in-trade to the franchisees. But in any new business development there will always be people looking for easy money and who may finish up being duped. Notwithstanding such human frailities, the system has many advantages to offer, both to the franchisee and to society and the economy as a whole. These are:

The franchisee
(*a*)   Has the vested interest of the entrepreneur.
(*b*)   Enjoys the benefits of full association with large operation.

(*c*)   Can obtain managerial advice and guidance.
(*d*)   Enjoys joint promotion and reputation.
(*e*)   Has a tried and proved system of operation.

The franchiser
(*a*)   Enjoys the self-motivation of the franchisee.
(*b*)   Expands his total distribution.
(*c*)   Limits his capital involvement.
(*d*)   Limits administrative problems involved.

Because both parties join their businesses together, the mutual benefits improve both firms' chances of success, with lowered investment risks, sounder decision-making and better use of joint resources. Perhaps the only real disadvantage of the system is that it may sometimes involve decisions made by the franchiser in the interests of the majority but which may be injurious to a few. All franchisees must ensure that they do not sign away real control of their business. For those individuals or organisations considering a franchise operation, the Institute of Marketing publishes a checklist available free.

4   After-sales service: installation, maintenance, service, spare parts

Few companies have realised the growth potential that exists through the development of a first-class after-sales service promoted as a pre-sale incentive. Volkswagen grew in America because of the company's insistence on minimum standards of operation among its distributors. The conditions were so stringent that they amounted to a legal franchise of the sort described earlier. Despite the renowned success of the operation, few companies have adopted a similar approach. Building foundations for tomorrow do not seem to appear high on the list of company priorities, hence the dearth of planning systems and the reluctance to develop customer service.

Even so, there is no reason why the company's own service staff should not receive promotional training. Like the salesman, the service engineer is in frequent contact with the customer. Unlike the salesman, however, he has to deal with the people responsible for running the machine *who will not have been sold on the machine's potential, its benefits and the reasons for its original choice.* It may have caused redundancies, loss of earnings, demotion. In resentment the machine's operation could be 'spiked' (concealed sabotage). The new owners will blame the suppliers. Even if they don't, goodwill may be harmed. A good engineer trained to understand machine/people problems will attempt to sell the merits of the machine and take pride in showing his counterpart how to get the maximum benefit. Because he is an engineer he will tend to feel somewhat shamefaced about a second-hand or an inexpensive model. In an efficient company he is taught that customers know best and buy what suits them. He is shown that with a cheaper machine customers can make profits, while with a bigger, more sophisticated piece of equipment – perhaps his own pride and joy – they may make thumping great losses if it has more capacity than can be economically used.

In making a capital investment a company rates 'troublefree' operation as highly as the average motorist, not just because servicing is expensive but because stopped machines make men idle, lower production, allow perishable raw materials to spoil and keep customers waiting. The resultant cost may be very high indeed. Building a reputation for 'trouble-free running' adds a premium value to the machine. Even if management does not acknowledge this real truth it is clear the trade unions have. They know the best time and place to strike.

In the motor car industry the manufacturers now recognise the need to carry a full range of spare parts, and Unipart campaigns have created an extended revenue-earning opportunity.

The rules adopted by service-orientated companies are:

(*a*)   After-sales service is a sales *promotional* function.
(*b*)   Installation is supplied in the price and expected to be fully and satisfactorily operational when the product is sold.
(*c*)   Maintenance is the means of safeguarding the company's reputation.
(*d*)   Service is the means of making a customer's investment pay.
(*e*)   Spare parts are an integral part of a piece of equipment and extras will be supplied automatically prior to MTBF (Mean Time Before Failure).

Clearly there is scope for improvement in most companies. The need is so apparent that some companies are making a successful business out of safeguarding customers' needs by renting, or leasing, goods such as television sets, cars, etc. and are therefore providing a full free and efficient service.

5 Customer guarantees and legal controls

All marketing transactions in the UK are subject to numerous Acts of Parliament, and ultimately the legal system. In a perfect world, all marketing companies would develop products and services to the point where they are so customer-orientated that recourse to the courts would be unnecessary. Similarly, in such a world consumers would be willing and able to conduct their transactions with discretion and honour. In the real world there is always conflict, although some companies have made a success of guaranteeing customer satisfaction or money back without question. Although some consumers abuse this concession, most customers are fair and the policy is mutually beneficial. In some circumstances the Parliamentary Acts and their enforcement are superfluous. For other companies the issue of warranties or guarantees must offer more benefits than are already contained within the relevant Acts, or they are worthless.

6 Stock control

In studying the annual accounts of numerous firms it seems that many of them are carrying excessive stocks. Dividing the stock-held value into the sales revenue for two or more successive years shows average stocks valued at many months of sales. This is true of companies with delivery lead times of weeks rather than months. Yet no doubt these companies are confronted with constant stock-out problems. They all seem to face a conflict involving the desirable mix of stock items. The conflict is between the need to satisfy customers' demands and the necessity to produce in economic batch quantities. So the supplier faces a double problem: when to produce, and how much to produce? These conflicting interests need to be considered in more detail. The benefits of holding stock are:

(*a*)   Lower average unit costs of production

(*b*)   More efficient production programming
(*c*)   Better delivery timing
(*d*)   Avoidance of excess scrap

Clearly stock-holding provides a cushion for both the manufacturer and his customer. The limiting of risk that this entails is, moreover, additional to the higher productivity achievable from the system. The evaluation of each kind of benefit is made easier by further consideration.

(a)   Lower average unit costs of production

By deciding economic batch quantities a company makes savings on each quantity made. The principle is similar to that applying to the theory of economies of scale. Machine set-up time is minimised, purchase order levels are realistic and timed, and, of course, the limiting factor of time is used to economic advantage.

(b)   More efficient production programming

If goods are made to order, then not only will more general-purpose machinery be required but also machines will be only partly used for production. More efficient production is achieved by running purpose-built machines at maximum capacity for long periods. By planning ahead the production manager is able to utilise the machines in this way by making for stock rather than dealing with each order as it arrives and deploying machines accordingly. This approach is particularly beneficial when goods have a seasonal demand. It is realised by the more progressive companies that limited output from machines must carry a higher rate of overhead per unit than units of mass production or economic production.

(c)   Better delivery timing

Delivery is an inherent feature of a purchase just as much as price or product specification. Extended delivery may force a customer to seek compensation for remaining loyal. Clearly 'ex-stock' is a desirable benefit to offer prospects, particularly if delivery can be made almost instantly. There is little point in building up large stocks if the delivery service is poor. Customers judge by actual delivery, not by the ex-works state. In fact, there is nothing more infuriating to a customer than to know that his urgent needs are available at the factory but that the delivery van is not due for two weeks.

(d)   Avoidance of excess scrap
Most products have a minimum output level. For example, a printer may offer to supply 100 printed leaflets, but his price will allow for the 400 that may be wasted. Not all firms are able to charge the realistic rate for small orders because they have no sensible means of knowing just what that rate is.

The disadvantages of holding stock are:

(*a*)   The actual costs involved
(*b*)   Limitation on providing flexibility

(a)   The actual costs involved
These costs may be quite considerable. Moreover, there are numerous ways in which they are incurred:

> Cost of interest on capital tied-up
> Cost of the space
> Cost of shelving or special packaging
> Costs of damage or deterioration
> Costs of pilferage
> Costs of insurance
> Costs of administration
> Costs of handling and labour
> Costs of obsolescence
> Costs of lost opportunity

Although these are real costs, they apply equally at each stage in the channel of distribution, so for society as a whole the practice of keeping buffer stocks all the way down the line has a multiplier effect.

(b)   Limitations on providing flexibility
Carrying stocks made in economic quantities forestalls the possibility of a company meeting individual customer requirements, since the cost of ad hoc orders becomes prohibitive. This means that the supplier is less likely to be attuned to changes in the market place.

Stock-holding is an area where nominal adherence to marketing principles is revealed. The marketing plan may specify concentration of effort on a growth sector of the market, offering products with growth potential to companies of a size capable of meeting the minimum order requirements. In practice the weaker company meets the requirements of everyone that sends in an order, fills unused capacity with whatever happens to turn up in the post and carries stock for the major accounts who 'would go elsewhere for their computers if they did not supply their pencils'. Under such action it is small wonder that 'marketing' opportunities are missed and marketing management considered unsuccessful.

7   Telephone selling

As we have seen earlier, personal calls by the salesman are expensive in both selling and non-selling time, besides which the limited time available to salesmen is best spent with customers who are substantial prospects and in the way that is most effective – personal contact. In a well-chosen territory with 100 prospects offering real potential, the salesman is fully occupied.

But there is much business available that does not justify the personal attention of the salesmen – after all, the mail order business thrives on a selling job carried out through the mail – and these prospects have to be cultivated. Some may be happy to send orders through the post, and for the very small account this is the ideal way of handling the business. On the other hand, some businesses require a more active approach, particularly if their trade is thriving. The sales effort in this case is often left to an inside salesman trained to use the telephone to its best advantage. The telephone has flexibility and a time-saving factor not realisable in either personal calls or postal communications.

Although the telephone is often used as a supplement to the salesman, it is sometimes used to complement his efforts. The inside salesman uses the phone to supplement his selling activity on low-priority calls and to complement his selling effort at desirable calls where the salesman may not be able to visit as often as he should. The system has become so sophisticated in some fields that a number of companies have achieved prominent market growth attributable to their use of telephone selling techniques. Examples are double glazing, cavity-wall insulation, insurance, media space or air-time selling and word processing.

The specific benefits attributable to the telephone are:

(a)   Low cost of frequent contact.
(b)   Is a time-saving factor for both parties.
(c)   Provides a filter on potential of prospects.
(d)   Can be used for promotions as well as order-sending.
(e)   Enables the sales person to meet objections.
(f)   Calls can be timed to meet customer needs.
(g)   Helps to improve market coverage.
(h)   Enables changes in price etc. to be conveyed immediately.
(i)   Is a check on the salesman's performance.
(j)   Enables high-calibre married women to be used more readily.
(k)   Solicits real leads for salesmen.
(l)   Allows re-call during times of pressure.
(m)   Makes use of standardised sales presentation possible.

These points make the use of the telephone a formidable promotional weapon and one that has considerable potential for all companies. Its blessing is that it is entirely modular and so allows big things to develop from small beginnings.

8   Premiums and joint ventures

The premiums promotions business has yet to get over its 'daffodil'. The scope for the promotional method is high. Many items if manufactured in bulk, perhaps in a once-off order, can be produced at a price significantly cheaper than if produced and marketed in a slow-moving market. Often the significant costs may be in distribution, and where 'carried' by some other item the additional costs may be minimal. In this way a manufacturer is often able to make premium offers for goods valued at £15 for, perhaps, £5·99. Special offers of this sort enable firms to provide excellent value for money to the consumer. And no one loses anything because an unexploited market has been tapped. As a promotional technique the premium promotion is particularly useful for:

(a)   Introducing a new product
(b)   Extending an existing market

(*c*)   Increasing usage
(*d*)   Building 'trade' goodwill
(*e*)   Special sales campaigns
(*f*)   Increasing order value
(*g*)   Weakening competitive activity
(*h*)   Monitoring publicity campaigns

One of the hidden benefits of running a premium promotion is the direct contact this introduces to the manufacturer. Apart from anything else it provides the concern with a mailing list, with which future promotion activity may be undertaken and used as a control document. But premium promotions are joint ventures. Joint ventures provide another useful channel of distribution, but equally they provide a means by which a company may extend the area of its service so prohibiting the growth of competitors.

9   The sales office organisation

Although the services provided by most offices tend to be similar, they are often organised in different ways:

(*a*)   Functional organisation
(*b*)   Product-based organisation
(*c*)   Market-based organisation
(*d*)   Area-based organisation
(*e*)   Integrated office organisation.

The organisation adopted by the firm is usually dependent on its corporate strategy – the means by which its marketing operation is implemented. As the office is usually the nerve centre of the business, further consideration of the different organisations is necessary.

(a)   Functional organisation

In this category an employee or group of employees performs the same function for all company products or sales. These functions will include handling inquiries, pricing, sampling, stock records, estimating, credit control, tendering, progress chasing and costing. Each employee must be sufficiently versatile to handle the range of tasks for which he or she is responsible.

(b)   Product-based organisation
In this type of organisation staff are recruited with 'product' knowledge, with each section largely self-sufficient and responsible for a particular product or group of products.

(c)   Market-based organisation
The staff in this organisation are divided up into sections, with each section responsible for a specific market, usually distinguished by a particular class of outlet. In this type of organisation the staff will be expected to have sound knowledge of the operational structure and procedures for the class of outlet for which they are responsible.

(d)   Area-based organisation
This type of organisation may be any permutation of the above, but with its geographical areas divided into territories capable of easy handling by office staff.

(e)   Integrated office services
The acceptance of computers and data processing has tended to break down departmental walls and so it is no longer necessary for the sales office to be separated from accounts or purchasing. In this organisation the office is fully integrated, with an office manager providing expertise in record-keeping, transcription and management information systems.

10   Enquiry handling

Every customer first became a customer as a result of an enquiry. Every customer wanting additional goods or services makes an enquiry. Every enquiry is a business opportunity. It is an organisation looking for supplies and prepared to pay for them. If business does not result from an enquiry, it must be because the supplier did not want the business. It should not, as so often happens, be by default. Many firms lose business because they do not respond adequately to the invitation. Either they delay replying or they do not trouble to establish the enquirer's real needs. While it is true that some firms will send out circular letters in the search for suppliers (indicating that something is wrong with the supplier's promotional efforts), it is more usual for a prospect to make contact with one of his established suppliers, possibly the salesman, and ask whether they know of a source. Because his reputation is at stake the supplier will recommend a firm known to him as reliable and efficient. Judgment will be based on what other customers have reported.

The only golden rules for enquiry handling are: use a system and make one person responsible, and issue a definite policy and procedure with monitoring of progress and results. And remember that many enquiries start with the telephone operator.

11   The sales supporting service

In the chapters covering the salesman and sales management it was emphasised that, because of the real cost of face-to-face selling time, considerable improvements in productivity may be achieved if the salesman is helped in the performance of his more routine functions. So apart from the sales office carrying out many routine calls by telephone, the clerical staff can be helpful in obtaining and supplying useful information to the salesman and his customers.

12   Management information, accounting, computers, operational research

While modern management techniques have been widely documented as aids to cost effectiveness, it is often forgotten that improvements in operating efficiency also benefit the customer.

Sales analysis may well indicate trends in market movements. Such information could be vital to a customer struggling to decide where to invest his capital for growth. Similarly, accounting information such as return on capital employed or return on sales could suggest more profitable opportunities, yet unknown to customers. This could be particularly true if it is discovered that customers are losing money because they are aiming for a high margin, so prohibiting growth. Cooperating with customers and supplying them 'below cost' until economies of scale are achieved could prove a wise investment compared with a heavy marketing campaign. Furthermore, computerisation, mathematical models and/or operational research techniques can be, and are sometimes, used to bring benefits to customers. Improving delivery schedules may often bring more rewards than reducing the operating costs of deliveries. This is true market- or customer-orientation. Using quantitative techniques often results in better decision-making data; they will be as vital to the future of marketing as qualitative techniques have been in the past.

12

Behavioural Aspects of Marketing

The study of behaviour may be related directly to the study of communications, for communications theory requires a full understanding of the drives, motives and aspirations of an individual or a group and therefore of an audience, a readership or a market. We live in an age of communications, with mass media telecommunications, satellites, electronics and data processing systems providing the means, and society the demand. Such demand may be seen to exist on purely logical grounds: for information, entertainment or education.

To marketing executives these are only manifestations of need. In modern marketing terms the real drives of the individual are for recognition, reward and romance. Successful communications, such as effective advertising, often appeal to one or more of these drives, although the appeal may not be immediately obvious. In a limited number of cases an appeal may be presented in such a way that people may not be able to recognise it at a conscious level. The subconscious, however, seems to have sharper senses and may accept the appeal unbeknown to the listener/viewer, so stimulating an interest or a favourable disposition towards the brand or service featured in the message This is one of the means by which society seems to have had its appetite for material acquisitions sharpened and developed aspirations for a higher standard of living. Marketing techniques are part of the process, as keys that will unlock natural resistance to change, overcome norms, values, attitudes or prejudices, and counter prudence, caution and restraint.

Although some people oppose the use of these techniques,

because they allegedly exploit people's weaknesses, it must be said that marketing practice does not create these weaknesses, but rather provides the means for their release and satisfaction. If the marketing approach fails, then the initial investment will be curtailed and the associated brand or service may disappear. Businessmen do not continue to invest in failure; that perhaps is the prerogative of those who are spending other people's money.

Gratification via the mass media

The mass media is the major means by which marketing communications are delivered. The different vehicles of mass media themselves provide behavioural satisfactions similar to those offered by advertisers. People in society may consciously turn to the media for information, entertainment or education, but in order to secure their reward, recognition or romance their individual media *needs* are quite different.

In an advanced society the standard of general education differs not only between the affluent and those of modest circumstances, but more significantly between the different generations. For although all share the benefits of modern technology, each generation has a wide disparity of educational levels and exposure to life experience. Many people were born before the advent of television and electronic gadgetry, for example, yet have experienced war.

To many people the mass media presents another reality: consider the anger or affection inspired by characters in serials or series. Such characters are the figment of a writer's imagination, yet to much of the population they are real people living their lives on the screen. Satisfying the needs of such people is not exploitation, but recognition of the demand, for although people know the programmes are fictitious, they react to them as if they were real. They are therefore creating a world in their minds that provides more satisfaction than the world in which they live. Marketing people add to that creation through advertising and promotional themes and schemes.

Researchers for IPC, seeking to establish the underlying role of the mass media, identified six uses or gratifications:

Diversion   The media provide the means by which people can escape from routine, personal problems and emotional stress. It eases the strain associated with pressures at work or in personal relationships.

Personal identity   It enables people to find common ground between situations and events in their own lives and those of others beyond the reach of normal everyday contact. It overcomes barriers of time or distance.

Inter-relationships   It provides individuals with substitutes for personal companionship and brings company to the lonely.

Social intercourse   By providing foundations in mutual knowledge, it enables individuals to establish easy communication with new acquaintances and so provides a basis for future friendship. It enables people to mix more easily.

Attitude association   It helps attitudes to be based on deeper understanding and so can enrich the quality of life. It makes for greater tolerance and consideration for others.

Reassurance   It helps to make people self-confident and encourages self-esteem through knowledge. It provides an indemnity against the problems of ignorance.

In understanding these uses and gratifications of the mass media, it is apparent that marketing techniques often satisfy people's psychological needs. A young man may buy a sports car in order to win the attention of the opposite sex. Females may not be impressed by his car, but they may well be attracted by the self-confidence he has assumed. It is for these reasons that we identify a brand or a service with both *substance* and *image*.

Substance is what the product is and does; *image* is what the buyer perceives it to be, or what he thinks it will do. So image is often associated with some deep-rooted satisfaction which goes beyond an apparent need. The perception of an individual is affected by past experiences and attitudes. In a society where past and present experience and attitude formation are largely influenced by a common service – the mass media – then individual perceptions may well reflect those of the majority. Where perceptions are predictable, an effective communication may be developed to appeal to the collective needs of the community. As the predicted perception will be based on a psychological need, it will elicit a known and desired response.

In this way a brand is offered to the public; it will have a quality or association which is known to appeal to the population and will be presented in such a way that it will be perceived favourably, whether at a conscious or subconscious level. This is the essence of good marketing: giving the consumers what they need, and offering it in a way that makes it easy for them to buy. So research has focused on establishing relationships between behaviour and underlying processes involving people's needs, their wants, aspirations, intentions and drives. The behavioural approach to marketing is now an established feature of modern management.

Characteristics of the behavioural sciences

Marketing management uses the behavioural sciences to increase marketing efficiency and to enhance the quality of its services to the community. This involves an understanding of attitudes, personality, level of sophistication, motivation, learning and cognition.

People's attitudes are a relatively stable set of opinions, interests or purposes which can be expected to produce a certain response to a given stimulation. Attitudes are formed by one's culture, environment and social groups. Extensive first-hand experience or even appropriate knowledge will not normally in themselves bring about a change in attitude. Similarly, attacks on attitudes will arouse hostility and a consolidation or justification of the original belief, to the extent that even an illogical approach may be adopted to retain the attitude held. Although it may be possible to modify an attitude or opinion held by an individual, it is not normally possible to do so among groups of people by the use of reason alone. Individuals will not adopt a new attitude which is likely to bring them into conflict with other members of their normal group. Changes of attitude may best be brought about therefore by communication to individuals collectively and by providing the means by which individuals can exert influence within their groups.

Personality is the unique integration of an individual's psychophysical systems that determine his or her behaviour and unify the individual's motives, values, beliefs, aspirations and feelings. The way to secure the desired response to a communication is to recognise the environmental conditioning of these psychophysical systems. Perhaps the most significant of these is the ego, the known and knowable self, a combination of one's learning, thinking and memory. Understanding these psychological processes, and how they function for each member of the population, is central to effective communication. How people are likely to react to a theme and how they will respond to psychophysical appeals may be the province of the copywriter, but will be significant also in the development of a marketing strategy consistent with the marketing concept, whether it be in products, communications or company philosophy. So in developing corporate policy and in projecting this into external communications, a company builds a bridge between its own needs, those of its shareholders and employees, and those of its customers, including both their material and psychological needs.

Effective communications and marketing knowledge are constantly evolving: the more sophisticated the marketing, the more sophisticated it needs to become. Radical marketing themes or schemes soon become commonplace and mediocre. This is also a feature of human or social development. Both move through stages or platforms, with each succeeding stage dependent on the preceding stage, but they require appropriate stimulation from the environment. In the age of communication nourishment is largely dependent on the mass media, and particularly so for adults. So levels of sophistication need the media in order to grow, while advertisers need the media so as to stimulate public awareness. They are becoming interdependent.

Continuing development in society depends on the collective motivations of its population. While the germ of motivation differs from one individual to another and its effects are virtually incomparable, their manifestations are almost common or universal. So the means of tapping them is clustered around basic appeals: those offering reward, recognition and romance.

Learning is a process of memory; learning theory is based on stimulated response, or cognitive theories. In either case there is an element of reward for achievement. So at an early age people are conditioned to expect some reward. As they mature, their need for nominal rewards expands. It soon requires attention from the opposite sex, and so romance, and, concurrently, a demand for recognition develops. Marketing practitioners use the learning process to bring knowledge of brands. By using learning theories, advertisers educate people to desire specific branded products. When these theories are skilfully applied, people become convinced of the benefits secured from particular brands, as a result of perception of image, and so an association of ideas between the brand and satisfaction is established.

It is in this way that a company earns a reputation monopoly and gains brand leadership. Such successful companies may secure a premium return on their initial investment, for even although their selling prices may be higher than their competitors', the reputation monopoly may create inelasticity of demand for the brands concerned.

Members of society tend to conform. They do not like conflicts and so try to avoid them. Similarly, they do not like inconsistencies, and where these arise there may be alteration in belief, in behaviour, or both. The theory of cognitive dissonance is based on the need for consistency. Cognitive means the act of knowing, perceiving or conceiving while dissonance refers to the jarring effect of tones which do not blend yet which are too close to be distinguished. Cognitive dissonance usually relates to the decision-making process where a decision automatically cancels alternatives. After making a buying decision, such as acquiring a particular new car, the buyer worries about the wisdom of his decision. Appropriate marketing action helps to overcome any such worry and will reinforce the buyer's decision.

Perception
People often see what they want to see, usually as a result of previous experiences or a developed sense of awareness. An association of ideas or values brings about a perception. In this way people may identify with a brand image and enter into a subconscious commitment to buy. Use of colour, personalities, shapes or symbols produces this association and so brings about a favourable disposition towards the brand concerned. Individuals, en masse, judge others by their voices, whether they be warm, sincere, confident or considerate. Actors adopt the required tone, add facial animation or body language, and so provide the appropriate impression. Music is a major part of effective communication, as it

provides atmosphere and can induce almost any human emotion. Thus when the required perception is identified, the appropriate behavioural theme established, and the necessary communication skills assembled, the mass media can convey the message to the selected target market.

The five human senses of sight, sound, touch, smell and taste are the basic means of effective communication. In transmission media it is necessary to project warmth, pain, cold or pressure by the use of simulation, with the required sensation coming from visuals of tropical heat, horror, arctic conditions, and from pulsating or throbbing images. Many people are so conditioned that even a hint of an aroma will bring forth a strong suggestion of a chosen fragrance, while taste buds are easily excited and mouthwatering may occur when pleasant memories are evoked. The principal kinds of taste are sweet, sour, bitter and salt, and selected words may be used to excite the required pleasurable sensations. Images are created in this way. In pure business terms, the promoted product must satisfy the perception or it will die commercially.

Classification of population groups

The classification of society into identifiable groups is essential to market targeting, and the socioeconomic groups suggested by the Institute of Practitioners in Advertising has long been established in the UK. These groups have been the principal classification base used by the mass media, together with age groupings and regional distribution. Attempts have been made to produce alternatives, but they are still the major classifications used by the UK mass media and continuous survey research organisations.

More recent attempts at classification have been prompted by the need to identify purchasing behaviour patterns. Lifestyles have provided the basis for one approach, while psychographic classifications have been suggested according to different personality types. The most notable successes have been achieved in classifying people into specific, almost psychogenic categories. For example, the toothpaste market may be divided into worriers about tooth decay, socialites concerned about fresh breath, beauticians preoccupied with whiteness, sensorisers looking for taste, and the economisers who buy only on price. Clearly, identifying these groups, emphasis-

The IPA Social Grades

Social Grade	Social Status	Occupations
A	Upper middle class	Higher managerial, administrative or professional
B	Middle class	Intermediate managerial, administrative or professional
C1	Lower middle class	Supervisory or clerical, and junior managerial, administrative or professional
C2	Skilled working class	Skilled manual workers
D	Working class	Semi and unskilled manual workers
E	Those at lowest level of subsistence	State pensioners or widows (no other earner), casual or lowest grade workers

ing an appropriate product benefit, and so establishing an image monopoly, is the essence of the behavioural approach to marketing. So from this point of view each brand will be aimed at, and bought by, people with a certain lifestyle, or by people with similar attitudes, values or aspirations.

A relatively new concept, ACORN, is based on the belief that people living within close proximity will have similar behaviour or purchasing patterns. ACORN has developed descriptions of these types, classified according to their housing conditions:

A   Modern family housing for manual workers
B   Modern family housing for higher incomes
C   Older housing of intermediate status
D   Very poor quality, older terraced housing
E   Rural areas
F   Urban local authority housing

G   Housing with most overcrowding
H   Low income areas with immigrants
I   Students and high status non-family areas
J   Traditional high status suburbia
K   Areas of elderly people

These types of classifications are increasingly being used as a means of research into cost-effective marketing action. The behavioural approach to marketing is to identify particular groups of society, to isolate those with a high propensity to purchase, to discover their likely motivations, and then to present an image of a brand that will appeal to their psychological or psychogenic needs. The techniques associated with these methods are heavily criticised by some people. However, the techniques continue to develop and succeed where others have failed, which suggests an acceptance, or even an endorsement, by society. Where they succeed, they bring satisfaction to consumers, jobs to the employees, and help the economic development of a country and of the world in general. They bring a better alternative to economic depression.

13

Brand Management

Throughout the long history of commerce, supplying or producing a product or commodity has been the dominant feature of trading. Making available goods that have been scarce where demand is strong and competition non-existent ensured a heavy concentration of resources on obtaining necessary supplies. In the free world where such investments have established excess capacity, suppliers now have to compete to secure customers. The pendulum has swung. Resources are now being concentrated on winning and holding custom. In the same way that technicians have worked on improving production methods to maximise output while minimising unit costs, specialists now study systems and procedures to improve the productivity of the marketing functions. Because economic manufacture, utilising mass production techniques, has concentrated output in large factories, and efficient financial management has accumulated extensive product ranges, the span of control makes heavy demands of marketing executives. Much executive efficiency has been achieved by delegation, a result of detailed planning, and by the use of specialist product managers. Meanwhile, improvements in the deployment of marketing activities have come from changes in marketing strategy and tactics. So the management of one or a limited number of products within the company range has become the province of the brand manager, while consideration of the appropriate marketing mix to ensure brand development or switching in changing conditions is the major preoccupation of these new style executives.

The use of branding is an important concept in marketing. A

company's brand name is a consumer franchise of considerable market value. The introduction and successful use of brand names has been a critical factor in the development of trading, and they are vital to many multinational companies throughout their international markets. A brand name identifies or distinguishes a product from those produced by its competitors. It allows the consumer to recognise the product on display or in advertising, and to expect a particular level or consistency of quality associated with its name. In this sense branding has a significance which is analagous to the hallmarking of gold and silver.

Branding offers advantages to all parties in the marketing chain. Manufacturers are able to exercise greater control over their promotions by stimulating demand-pull for their brand. A brand name is the essence of communication, not only for identification, but for the theme of an advertising campaign, whether introducing the product or maintaining its sales momentum.

By investing in demand-pull promotions the manufacturer helps wholesalers and retailers. He relieves these distributors of the major selling role, so enabling them to concentrate on merchandising the branded product. By efficient brand promotions consumers are attracted in advance, and their prior decision-making ensures rapid traffic flow through retail outlets and distribution through warehouses. Brand names help the distributors in ordering and stock control, and the retailer in layout and display.

For the consumer, a brand name means a guarantee of quality, easy recognition while shopping, and the confidence that comes with repeat purchasing. A brand name also provides the basis for the development of a brand image and the possibility of establishing a sound reputation monopoly. Brand names may be associated with the parent company's name, such as Phillips, Black & Decker, or Heinz. In some cases they may be contrived names, such as Eastman's Kodak, Marks & Spencers' St Michael, or Cadbury's Smash. Sometimes manufacturers make use of well-known names of personalities or characters, but often the most successful technique is to use appropriate descriptive terms: those that are short and easy to pronounce and have pleasant associations. They should be easy to remember, such as Crest, Tide or Frigidaire.

The brand manager

The brand manager, who may be called the product manager in some industrial marketing companies, combines a line and a staff function. He or she will have a profit responsibility similar to that of a managing director of a small firm, but will also have to undertake all of the intellectual theorising of the planner. He must organise research into the market and the product, prepare forecasts and budgets, and establish a pricing policy that will maximise profitability. He is held accountable for a profit centre.

The brand man, as he is sometimes called, has to decide between a policy of high volume and the competitive price to achieve it, or an upmarket price that will bring a high profit ratio. In some cases the decision may be determined by pressure in the market place, or conversely by the image the company has initiated as marketing policy. He will plan the communications mix, and develop the brand's appropriate marketing mix.

In modern organisations, line managers hold considerable responsibility and a firm's complex workings requires trained and experienced specialists. Production managers may be engineers; accountants will have had years of experience and functional responsibility. Within the marketing department are specialists in public relations, market research, advertising, merchandising or packaging. Each of the specialists has a different view of the company's priorities. Each will often believe his own department has the necessary skills or resourcefulness to tackle current or future issues. In particular each functional department sees problems for the company as a whole. They do not necessarily see nor fully understand the particular needs or problems of individual brands, but where they do they are confronted with competing demands or conflicts of interests among brands. In order to overcome these problems, each brand manager strives to win confidence in and priority for his brand. In this way every brand has the most comprehensive consideration and yet has to stand the test of direct comparison with all competing claims for company resources. In undertaking this task the brand man coordinates all of the activities of the marketing spectrum.

Coordinating often diverse and usually diffuse activities requires not only skill, but facts: to clarify complex issues, to enable decision-making, to highlight opportunities or problems, or even to plan necessary remedial actions. The key words for the manager are *what*, *where*, *when*, *who*, *why* and *how*. Armed with facts, he can make positive proposals, organise campaigns, make decisions and monitor the results of his marketing actions. He analyses trends and compares the performance of one activity against another. He commissions his own fact-finding research and obtains reports and studies from the major continuous research survey organisations.

Although it is a comparatively easy matter to discover the cluster of satisfactions required by the consuming public for an existing or new product, the brand manager will still have to devise a total proposition or offer that will attract customers from the target audience. Products are normally bought by brand name or image, or by the reputation of the producer or seller. The brand manager, in consultation with his marketing team, must find the appropriate image that will become the core of all marketing activity. It is in this area that many managers have brought success to well-known companies, and often achieved market leadership and high profitability in the face of near-homogeneous brand competition. However, the nature of marketing is such that successes are easy to attribute after the event. Probably there are more failures, but these are not brought into the spotlight. Common to the success of many brands is the attention to planning from which an image evolves and becomes accepted by the community, or perhaps simply emerges and is then pursued by the supplying company.

The planning abilities of the brand manager which lead to successful promotions are:

To recognise a sound marketing plan
To understand the problem areas of brand marketing
To coordinate a plan with other functions
To develop and monitor forecasts and budgets
To carry responsibility for implementation
To acknowledge the need for modification
To create enthusiasm for the plan
To organise brand strategy
To originate plans for the communications mix
To prepare capital investment plans
To absorb details of economic conditions

To analyse supporting brand reports

To have a clear understanding of people, their behaviour patterns, drives and motivations

These are the special requirements of brand managers, and so suggest the qualities needed by the right person for the job. Such people will normally be trained on the job, but will also have undertaken some formal study leading to a qualification such as those provided by the Institute of Marketing and the CAM Foundation in the United Kingdom. Brand management serves as a critical organisational function in large concerns, and it provides the level of responsibility and experience necessary for promotion to senior positions. Many senior marketing managers owe their present status to abilities developed as brand managers, often with other firms.

Product differentiation

While emphasis has been given to differentiating a brand by abstract appeals to the emotions many companies rely successfully on other marketing strategies. Some practise non-differentiating marketing. Advertising appeals are made by simply providing entertainment as a reminder of the brand. Normally such brands are well-known and little can be said that has not already been presented to the market.

Some companies offer a unique functional advantage with their product; the advantage is associated with that brand and no major competitor attempts to copy the brands distinction. They prefer to appeal in their own way to other segments in the market.

In some markets a company concentrates all of its promotion on quality superiority as a differentiating feature. They sell exclusively on prestige, although the product must live up to the image it is given or is perceived to have.

Whatever the differentiation given it must not fail the consumer. Obviously, the abstract is less likely to fail because it cannot, by definition, be measured. But as a product, with a utility or function, it must not fail.

Products launched on purely psychological grounds alone will not normally succeed. The Strand cigarette was launched with the theme 'You are never alone with a Strand'. Its appeal was to the basic loneliness in every human being, but obviously aimed at smokers who are believed to rely on cigarettes as an emotional crutch. The advertising campaign was brilliantly executed, but the product failed. It had no discernable differentiation and failed because in the absence of a genuine product benefit it had to rely on the theme of loneliness. While all people may have periods or moments of loneliness, they do not normally advertise the fact. So the act of purchasing a Strand cigarette or offering them around would be a public statement of loneliness. With hindsight it is possible to indicate why failure was certain, yet highly professional marketing men were involved and little criticism was expressed by other observers during the product's brief life span. So loneliness as a theme joined the band of human frailties which are taboo to blatant exploitation, such as fear or religious belief. Such appeals may work, but they have to be subtle.

While a real product benefit may lead to a theme for promotional purposes, not all marketing organisations agree on concentrating on just one feature of a product for marketing purposes. Some believe that providing details of a wide range of benefits will suggest a total package to some buyers, while people with a particular need will be able to find from the range featured the one most applicable to them. It can be said that the concentration on one benefit helps to establish a monopoly over that benefit, but limits the range of appeal. Featuring a number of benefits broadens the appeal, but does not provide for a unique selling proposition. Yet decisions on which benefits to feature may be determined by the choice of advertising media. Television, radio, cinema or posters may limit the focus to only one benefit, while the press is more suitable for showing a wide range of product benefits.

Product policy

While the brand manager is concerned with the profitability of one brand, the marketing manager and his management colleagues are preoccupied with the whole product range. This has the most direct influence on profits of any management activity and few problems demand more constant management attention. Functional managers are making decisions almost daily that affect the product range directly or indirectly. Priorities on sales efforts, promotional campaigns, production schedules, batch quantities, cash flow, inventory, storage, distribution and warehousing affect products differently, so individual profit contributions vary. Introducing new products and milking or terminating established ones may be critical to the company. Often a company has evolved its own list of the characteristics most likely to prove successful in products, and also those characteristics that experience has shown will not normally succeed. Thus it is possible for certain companies to succeed with particular products where others will fail. This knowledge helps to establish a formal product policy within the firms. It is in this way that companies are able to make product decisions easily and rapidly, because the product policy epitomises a company's business philosophy and its long-term strategy. It enables lower and middle management to pull together within a framework of common knowledge and understanding. The policy provides for an awareness of profit and performance expectation, and therefore aids in the development of revenue forecasts and budgeted costs. Part of the product policy will be devoted to company objectives, in marketing, sales, advertising and media, and will provide for sound direction and coordination towards a common goal. Out of such formalisation of company product policy will have evolved a unique set of characteristics that give rise to a corporate personality. The projection of that personality is central to the company's future prospects in the market place. Making decisions about such projections involves brand managers in the selection and the constitution of appropriate marketing activities.

The marketing mix

Although senior management will be concerned with the development of company objectives and its commercial philosophy, it is normally brand managers, with a profit centre responsibility, who develop marketing strategies for their brands within the framework established by marketing management. So once a target market is established, a means of winning the patronage of that market has to be devised. In many cases the means may be determined by the type or composition of the target market. The brand manager will have a profile of his potential market with information on propensity to purchase, i.e. the level of effective demand by different groups, the type of costs involved in the media reaching them, the outlets they normally use, the sort of appeals they will respond to, and the extent to which they are likely to respond to such appeals.

This process of market segmentation will include details of competitive activity and of any gaps that may exist in the services already provided – the gap analysis approach to market studies. The profile will include details of those market segments which the company is best able to serve because of its own established reputation and image, its effective distribution network and its established marketing strengths. In some cases the profile will include details of market segments that the company would wish to serve, because of their purchasing power, size, growth rate, location or influence, and new products that may provide entry to such markets may well be given some priority. The first step in marketing is to determine the primary target market, while also identifying possible secondary markets. The second step is to exploit it. Establishing the appropriate marketing mix, usually unique to each company, is fundamental to strategy, and is the translation of product policy needs into action.

The marketing mix will normally include:

Product mix	**Communication mix**
Product line range	Advertising
Design concept	Sales literature
Colour appeal	Field sales force
Style intention	Telephone sales
Package proposal	Public relations
Brand name	Direct mail
Price structure	Merchandising
Service function	Sales promotion
Warranty offer	

Distribution mix

(a) *Physical distribution*	(b) *Distribution channels*
Supplies	Retailer
Stock	Direct
Handling	Multiples
Storage	Wholesalers
Transportation	Overseas distributors
Warehousing	Direct export
	Trading blocs

Incentives mix

Money off	Premiums
Competitions	Pack offers.

The specific objectives for deciding the exact elements of the marketing mix may be to achieve a given return on investment, to stabilise a current market penetration, to realise a specific market share, or to overcome competition. These apply whether products in the market are virtually homogeneous or where some product differentation suggests a potential reputation monopoly. Normally, market segmentation is used where increased penetration is required into a specific target area, whereas companies relying on product differentiation will operate by trying to appeal to a broad market demand, but with limited penetration.

Marketing executives understand that deployment of the elements of the marketing mix requires careful coordination. To mount an extensive advertising campaign without ensuring effective distribution, or to cut prices without taking account of retailers' stock levels, could prove disastrous. Similarly, retailers are becoming irked at the number of money-off coupons in use and will sometimes allow the discounted amount provided to be set off against the customer's total bill, so allowing the consumer to benefit without the supplier achieving his promotional objectives. In developing the appropriate marketing mix, the brand manager or his equivalent will take account of the market forces in operation, behavioural aspects of target audiences, and the resources, strengths and weaknesses in both his own company and competitors', together with those of distribution channels. He or she will then juggle with the elements in the marketing mix in order to arrive at a cost-effective approach to meet company marketing objectives.

14

An Approach to Case Study Analysis

A case study is the presentation of a particular company with specific problems. Sometimes the available data may be abundant, yet the cases used rarely contain all the information the student would like. This is consistent with business practice, for information is usually expensive to secure and often time-consuming to gather. Sometimes the available data may even be superfluous.

Marketing practice is recognised by its 'cosmetic' appearance. It involves the annual expenditure of thousands of millions of pounds in the UK and its counterparts throughout the industrialised world. Cosmetic marketing may account for some 90% of all identifiable marketing expenditure and yet is ideally the end product of marketing management and practice, accounting for as little as 10–15% of actual marketing time. Sound and cost-effective cosmetic activity is normally dependent on diagnostic marketing – the process of finding out, understanding and establishing appropriate marketing performance.

The marketing audit is the means by which diagnostic activities are undertaken in order to establish any appropriate cosmetic action. This chapter provides a series of checklists covering the major aspects of the diagnostic approach, and a further series of checklists covering the areas for cosmetic activity.

The idea behind a case study is to simulate a real situation and so provide students with decision-making experience. A case is a vehicle for the identification of commercial problems, for analysing the relevant data, devising possible solutions and suggesting the likely problems associated with the implementation of these solutions. In general the businessman has tended to concentrate on trying out possible solutions – cosmetically – rather than getting to grips with real issues through diagnostic marketing. Students on the other hand often spend all of their time carrying out analysis, and then present a thin solution without qualifying their decisions and sometimes ignoring altogether the problems of implementing the chosen course of action. It is critical that the results of a case study analysis should persuade an examiner that the proposed solution makes commercial sense. There is no ideal solution nor any one acceptable answer, however.

It is important for students to understand that there will be no right or wrong answers to a case. Suggested solutions may be ranked according to the degree of appropriate analysis, the extent to which problems are identified and understood, the different possible solutions considered, and the final recommendation, together with the suggested methods of overcoming possible problems associated with the recommendation. In business the perfect solution will never be known. The decision to go ahead with a project automatically eliminates alternatives and it is never known for sure if the choice made is the best possible, no matter how successful it proves to be.

Although every case is different, and each firm's particular problems are unique, there is a format that will often be followed by individual company 'doctors'. In most cases the audit will start with the accounts. Studying the balance sheet and profit/loss accounts over a period, usually by some form of ratio analysis, often suggests changes in the balance of revenues and expenditures. In general there are only six ways of improving company profitability:

Increasing sales
Increasing prices
Reducing expenditure
Reducing capital investment
Changing the product mix
Changing distribution channels

Diagnostic marketing analysis of a case study will identify possible problems, to which cosmetic marketing activity may provide a solution.

When the case is first received the student should read it through from beginning to end in one relaxed sitting, but with an open mind. At this stage no attempt should be made to spot strengths or weaknesses, problems or even possible solutions. Any attempt to do this will condition the mind, and it becomes extremely difficult to change after this early conditioning. The immediate objective is to become acquainted with the situation and circumstances. After this initial reading, the case should be put aside for at least a day, resisting all temptation to grapple with issues. At this stage it may be advisable to take a photocopy. The photocopy may then be used as an observation platform for thoughts, ideas, comments or issues which can be annotated in red.

The next step is to set aside an afternoon or evening without interruption. On this occasion it is necessary to try and master the facts and to identify opinions provided in the case: these should be underlined in red on the photocopy. Facts and opinions almost invariably involve people, resources and the commercial environment. Make a note of all these issues separately.

Operational checklist

1   Read report briefly to become aware of total picture.
2   Study report closely, identifying explicit and implicit strengths, weaknesses, problems, opportunities and suggested solutions.
3   Analyse all data, looking for major problems and hidden opportunities. Such analysis may involve quantitative techniques.
4   Consider all behavioural possibilities within the organisation, taking into account the calibre of management, staff and work force. Assess motivation and informal group structures. Note any suggestion of a power structure or hierarchy.
5   Examine available and possible resources and any constraints or limiting factors. In particular, look at available finance and seek cost-effective activities.
6   Establish the format for a marketing plan; forecasts and budgets will be necessary.
7   Set profit, cash flow, marketing, selling, advertising and media objectives. Objectives are essential. Relate and coordinate all marketing communications channels. Many cosmetic marketing activities originate from communication problems.

8 Formulate budgets, forecasts, quotas. Business has one common denominator – money – so all recommended actions must be expressed in financial terms.

9 Provide detailed recommendations for action, including any limiting factors, planned contingencies, and how the resulting problems may be overcome.

10 List reasons for the recommended courses of action, with supporting arguments. It is necessary to rationalise and to justify all decisions.

11 Make any reasonable assumptions and give their justification. Examiners allow the use of reasonable assumptions, both to support recommendations and to qualify proposed actions.

12 Suggest any considered alternatives to that finally recommended and the reasons for their rejection. Indicate if any of these alternatives are possible contingencies.

13 Produce projections of expected results and justify resource requirements to achieve the relevant objectives.

14 Indicate necessary control procedures, including suggested monitoring devices, whether internal or external.

15 Make full use of diagrams, illustrations and checklists; it is necessary to persuade, and the use of advertising communications techniques is an essential marketing ploy, both in management and in business activity. They are no less valuable in communications to examiners.

A guide to quantitative analysis

Advanced case studies will invariably involve analysis of data by quantitative techniques. In general, data will involve comparisons (e.g. by ratio analysis) or trends (e.g. time series). The student should consider the following techniques, where appropriate, in the cases provided.

Comparative techniques

Breakeven analysis	Cash flow
Marginal costs/incremental analysis	Cost analysis
	Contribution analysis
Discounted cash flow techniques, net present value	Credit control
	Concentration analysis

| Ratio analysis | Economic batch quantities |
| Variance analysis | Linear programming |

Trend analysis
(Graphical expression may highlight problems or opportunities.)

% Return on capital employed	Profit per employee
% Return on sales revenue	Debtors ratio
% Sales on capital employed	Creditors ratio
% Stock on sales revenue	% Profits against fixed assets
Stockturn ratios	Liquidity ratios
%Production to sales	Capital gearing
% Marketing costs to sales	Operating ratios
% Administration costs to sales	Price/earnings ratios
Sales revenue per employee	Profit/volume ratios

Operational analysis

The areas where the bulk of marketing problems may be found are:

Sales revenue	Demand elasticity
Sales volume	Competitive strategy
Gross profit	Marketing communications channels
Net profit	Marketing mix
Major marketing expenses	Channels of distribution
Segmentation analysis	Advertising media cost-effectiveness
Geographical analysis	
Time series analysis	Production capacity
Comparative analysis	Pricing strategy
Market shares	Company philosophy
Brand performance	Competitive advantage
Market growth	

Planning considerations

All recommendations should be incorporated into a formal plan. Following a pattern of development, it is possible to prepare a marketing plan in a logical order. The actual measures that will normally comprise the plan are:

| Development of objectives | Appraisal of competitor profiles |
| Preparation of the sales forecast | Analysis of market shares |

Control of distribution
Schedule of publicity
Organisation of personnel
Arrangement of budgets
Provision of contingencies
Realisation of plan
Introduction of products
Operation of pricing decisions
Establishment of customer service

Evaluation of media
Deployment of public relations
Supervision of incentive marketing
Utilisation of packaging
Management of brands
Collection of marketing information
Administration of controls

The requirements of a plan

To be successful a plan must be organised into an agreed framework. A general format for a marketing plan is shown later. The essential requirements for such a plan are:

1 It must have an objective.
2 It must be expressed in simple terms.
3 It must provide for measurement.
4 It must provide for contingencies.
5 It must make effective use of resources.
6 It must have a common denominator – money.
7 It must specify responsibility of executives.
8 It must contain target completion dates.
9 It must include departmental activity tags.
10 It must inspire action.

Marketing planning, like the other activities of the marketing mix, has the distinction in commerce of being a dynamic element in the business operation. Planning is dynamic because it provides a compulsive force for:

1 The determination of real goals.
2 The exploration of different markets and the latent potential necessary to achieve real goals.
3 The systematic evaluation of the different product ideas needed in those markets
4 A choice of marketing strategy appropriate to achieve anticipated market sales potential.
5 The consideration of the best type of organisation to exploit the situation.

6   The adoption of a monitoring system relevant to the chosen commercial operation.

This compulsive force indicates the real and lasting value of the modern planning process; the true benefits of planning come from the purely conceptual and mechanical effort needed to establish and maintain a plan. The thinking through of problems and the fullest consideration of the management consequences following the introduction of any of the different remedial measures available provide the basis for success. In planning, the rewards come from what is put into the plan rather than from what is eventually published.

Planning controls
1   Is the market potential worth the effort?
2   Could the effort be better spent on other products?
3   Is the product group recently launched?
    (*a*)   Higher than expected launching cost?
    (*b*)   When is it expected to be profitable?
    (*c*)   Controls to ensure it is on target?
4   Can prices be raised
    (*a*)   Selectively?
    (*b*)   Overall?
5   Can production cost be reduced (with cheaper components, for example)?
6   Have possible reasons for internal ineffectiveness been examined?
7   What would be the effect on profitability of reducing marketing effort on this product (either total or altering marketing mix)?
8   Is range width or depth excessive?
9   Can small buyers be eliminated (or a minimum order charge introduced)?
10 What is profitability, by customer group or type?
11 If the product group is eliminated, what happens to fixed costs?
12 Is the product group substantially independent of others?
13 Could the product group be profitable in another environment?

The economic market

All industrial societies are subject to varying rates of growth or prosperity year by year. These variations happen because each period has a different set of conditions influencing the total outcome for the period. For the individual firm – and modern marketing companies are no exception – there are changing conditions, some of which may be beneficial, others that may not. Those that amount to obstacles for the firm to surmount are known as countervailing forces, and those that will normally improve the opportunities for a firm are known as prevailing forces. The following is a list of market forces, which may be countervailing or prevailing, according to circumstances:

Competition
Consumer memory lapse
Sales resistance
Market attrition
Social attitudes
Government legislation
State of the economy
Seasonal influences
Self-denial (e.g. dieting)
Industrial action
Industrial productivity
Personal sophistication
Developing mass media

Distribution of income
Relatively stable economy
Development of service
  industries
Provision of leisure
  pursuits
Range of choice
Redistribution of labour
Materialism
Age distribution
Planned obsolescence and
  standardisation
Credit/HP facilities

The most significant prevailing forces appropriate to modern marketing companies are extensions of these macro-economic considerations and, translated into more immediate demands as expressed and felt by people in our society today, are:

1 A demand for convenience
2 A search for labour-saving systems
3 A need for economy
4 A search for better lifestyles
5 A desire to overcome cognitive dissonance

In all case study analysis, appropriate consideration should be given to economic indicators at national and international levels.

The market information system

The criterion for securing good answers to market problems is to ask the right questions. The market plan will need to contain the reasoned solutions to the sort of problems likely to arise. The essence of planning therefore is to anticipate possible problems and to work out solutions *before* such problems arise.

The plan must contain basic information and data upon which reasoned solutions may be based. The minimum contents for the plan should be:

Market trends
Product profiles
Customer profiles
Product marketing strategies
Advertising environment
Selling environment
Advertising strategy
Advertising tactics
Media selection
Advertising theme or scheme
New products
Marketing overheads
· Marketing variables
Sales forecasts

Objectives
Corporate objectives
Marketing objectives
Advertising objectives
Distribution objectives
Selling objectives
Handling objectives

Segmentation of market
By product or product group
By territory
By demographic profile
By psychographic description

Selling activities
Inquiries obtained
Quotations submitted
Orders obtained
Cost per interview
Cost per call
Average value per order
Average gross profit per order
Local advertising costs
Number of canvassing calls
Average mileage per journey
Ratio of customers to prospects
Number of accounts opened

Market planning promotions
Establish promotional brief
Identify appropriate brand name
Write product description
Decide selling price
Analyse acceptance tests
Compare with competitive terms
Compare with substitute products
Make market evaluation
Establish market size
Decide likely prime gender usage

Forecast product life
Prepare consumer profiles
Decide geographical coverage
Consider market determinants
Assess advertising expenditure
Consider media split
Prepare budget
Phase advertising expenditure
Make seasonal weightings
Make regional weightings
Decide length of spots/size
  of space
Select day of week/time of day
Match required target
  audience to ratings
Summarise product
  advantages/benefits
Allay product disincentives
Build a unique selling
  proposition

**Advantages and limitations of
each product**
Appearance and presentation –
  packaging, size, quantity,
  quality, width of line,
  importance of brand name.
Consumer/user appeal –
  consideration of competitive
  prices, particular product
  benefits, prospects, general
  or special needs, the appeal
  to buying motives
Importance to the company –
  how many other items sold,
  the relationship of product
  to total sales, significance
  to image, relevance to
  company future policies

For each case study the student is given the role of decision-maker and will be expected to reason through each stage, function, activity and decision. The student should avoid the temptation to generalise without qualification: to suggest increasing sales, or mounting a promotional campaign, without suggesting why and how is meaningless. In fact, the student should be asking the questions why and how throughout the case study analysis, before applying these questions to all possible solutions.

In many case studies solutions may appear obvious. Such cases should be studied with great care. Not only are obvious solutions traps for the unwary, but they disguise the fact that making companies profitable may require quite minor changes, with many possible ways of making the changes effective.

In business management colleagues will have their own convictions on how problems may be overcome. Success depends on presentation of ideas, simply expressed, logically argued and strongly reinforced. These ideas stem from diagnostic marketing.

15

An Introduction to Quantitative Techniques

Quantitative analysis in marketing nearly always involves *comparisons* and/or *trends*. Because marketing executives are concerned with establishing cost-effective operations, they analyse the productivity of people, money and assets together with economic and environmental influences. So they compare the efficiency of their operations, markets, brands and employees one against another. They compare also profits, sales revenues and costs throughout their functions, and measure them against predetermined targets, budgets or quotes. The techniques they may use will include averages, measures of dispersion, sampling, probability ratios and significance tests. Because comparative studies will usually be made at one date – annually (often at the end of an accounting period), quarterly, monthly or weekly – such figures are shown vertically. But marketing executives are concerned also with decision-making, and many decisions involve a study of the past and then an extrapolation into the future. Thus trends are shown over a period of time and are therefore presented horizontally.

A manager's main task is to apply specific resources to achieve specified objectives. The availability and choice of resources is often limited by financial constraints (even though individual managers may have considerable discretion within present parameters), and the use of quantitative techniques provides an objective basis for decision-making. Chapter 12 identified areas and ideas where subjective thinking may be applied, yet the psychological approach is determined by quantitative analysis of society, social trends and behaviour. Similarly, the modern marketing manager will use objective investigation, and often the resulting evidence will indicate that a subjective approach is appropriate in order to persuade. For example, a statistical analysis of a market segment showing distinct behavioural patterns may suggest an advertising campaign aimed at a particular target audience, reading, viewing or listening to certain media, shopping in a definable geographical area, and making use of one type of retail outlet. So the appeal in the advertising may be purely emotive, yet the campaign will involve a major diagnostic study. It would therefore be highly objective yet involve a subjective application.

The techniques described, briefly, in this chapter have been selected from a wide range as being the most relevant to the marketing executive. For a full account of the concepts and mathematical calculations involved in their application, the reader should consult a text on business statistics and management accounting.

Measures of dispersion
In order to compare one distribution of data against others, to amplify the average and to establish just how representative it is of the group, it is necessary to measure its dispersion or spread. There are several methods available, of which the most useful is the *standard deviation* – this is found by taking the average of the squares of the deviations from the arithmetic mean, and then finding the square root of the sum of the squared deviations.

Regression analysis
Businessmen are always in search of data or information that will provide guidance on the likely outcome of some other important marketing activity. For example, a measure that will indicate the volume of sales that will result from any given level of advertising expenditure would be invaluable to marketing executives.

When measuring the relationship between two series of values businessmen often use an elementary regression line. The *method of least squares* is the most commonly used technique for determining the exact position of the line. This enables forecasts to be made from the line or path so established, for example to predict rates of growth.

Breakeven analysis

Breakeven analysis is a technique for studying the relationships among fixed costs, variable costs and profits. In all firms where investment in plant and machinery, management and staff, or marketing involves a minimum prior outlay and where the costs are incurred whatever the volume of trading, it follows that a certain amount of business has to be transacted, and a surplus earned above the variable costs, to recover the costs of these investments before a profit can be made. The point at which fixed costs and variable costs are recovered is the breakeven point. Clearly the selling price affects the point of breakeven and so different breakeven points may be calculated according to the selling prices considered and the resultant revenue and volume at each price level.

Ratio analysis

For effective control, management studies the trends over time of all the elements in the marketing budget. Although the results of such studies are often revealing, whether up or down or by variance from forecast, the information becomes significant when all the elements are considered in relation to each other. For example, increasing sales revenue may not be so attractive if bad debts or slow payers increase to the point where profits from the improved revenue are eroded as a result of the losses now being incurred. Comparison of the elements in budgets are normally by *relative* rather than *absolute* figures, so percentages or ratios are used. For many firms, ratios are the most useful because they provide for external comparison with other organisations and comparison against commonly accepted control ratios.

Moving average and moving annual total

In all businesses, sales, production and costs vary week by week and month by month. Any particular increase or decrease may not in itself be significant, as over a period of time such variations may be compensating. Marketing executives need to know whether changes are indicative of fundamental problems, however, and so use techniques to minimise the significance of variations in the short term and to establish underlying trends.

One of the most practical applications of the principle of the moving average is the *moving annual total* (MAT), where a fixed period – twelve months – is continually studied. This method enables the executive to 'smooth' the data and see the trend of the business, even if seasonal patterns occur or where, say, ordering patterns may be irregular in the short term but show much more consistency over longer periods of time. The longer the period studied, the more fluctuations are minimised; but the shorter the period, the more current are changes in the pattern.

Coefficient of correlation

A *correlation* is a measure of the relationship between variables – the *Pearsonian coefficient* is normally used to establish the degree of closeness between two sets of data, while the *rank coefficient* may be used to assess the degree of correlation between preferences, or between anticipated and actual preferences (e.g. in a survey). The degree of correlation may be positive (i.e. the trend for both sets of data lies in the same direction), zero (i.e. there is no relationship) or negative (i.e. one variable moves in the opposite direction to the other), and the range of measurement is from -1 for negative to $+1$ for positive correlation. In some cases a correlation may begin by being positive and finish by being negative: this is known as a *curvilinear correlation*.

One of the most useful marketing applications of correlation is in establishing a quantitative relationship between, say, advertising expenditure and sales income.

Probability distributions

In statistics it is possible to take the expression 'in all probability' a stage further than an exercise in judgment. Because statisticians have derived a number of standard theoretical probability distributions, it is possible to apply an appropriate distribution to a limited amount of data and so discover quantified probabilities of other possible outcomes.

The *normal distribution* provides an exact measure of distances of the standard deviation (see above) from the arithmetic mean. For example, 68% of all values of the variable are within the range of plus or minus one standard deviation from the mean of the distribution. Thus the normal distribution would enable, say, a clothing manufacturer to establish the likely demand for a range of sizes where the mean and the standard deviation of the population is known.

Many business operations involve a result of one of two possible outcomes – an order is won or lost, for example – and the *binomial* may be used to establish the probability of success or failure in a given number of trials where past rates of success or failure are known. The guidelines for using the binomial are that events are independent and that there is no pattern in the way in which successes or failures occur. Where a substantial sample of events is being studied, it is possible that the binomial probability distribution will match that of the normal distribution.

Although the *Poisson distribution* is a form of binomial, it has sufficient use to be considered a valuable distribution in its own right. It is particularly useful where the number of possible units is large and the probability small, where the use of the binomial would require much tedious calculation.

The normal, binomial and Poisson distributions are standardised and available as tables. Applying the appropriate data to the tables, much like logarithm tables, enables the executive to read off from the tables an indication of the likely outcome of any particular event. In essence, it is possible to predict the most likely outcome of an event, provided a minimum amount of data is known already.

Tests of significance

Significance tests, such as *Chi-square*, are used to determine whether or not the data provided by any sample of the population will allow a hypothesis to be assumed. If a test of significance for sampling error provides a null hypothesis, then it shows that any appreciable change or difference between expected and actual observed values is the result of an additional stimulus. It is possible, therefore, using a significance test, to establish whether any marketing action, such as advertising, has in fact caused any change in the market place, whether it be in awareness or purchasing behaviour.

Appendix
Examination Questions

The author and publishers are grateful to the Institute of Marketing (IM), the London Chamber of Commerce and Industry (LCCI) and the Communication, Advertising and Marketing Education Foundation (CAM) for permission to reproduce questions from past examination papers.

1 What functions does marketing comprise?   (IM Cert.)
2 What is the difference between *marketing* a product or service and *selling* a product or service?   (LCCI)
3 'Profit is the main function of marketing.' In what circumstances can this be shown not to be the case? Illustrate your answer with at least two examples.   (CAM)
4 In what ways do the goals of producers and consumers differ? (IM Cert.)
5 'What people need is one thing; what they buy is often quite another.' What does this imply for the marketer?   (IM Cert.)
6 Industrial Marketing may broadly be broken down into four main areas. Identify these and say how you think the marketing plan for each might vary.   (CAM)
7 Marketing principles suggest that the fact that a marketing programme is successful in one country gives little reason to suppose that it will be equally successful in another. Give a few of the major reasons why this should be so and show what practical steps can be taken to overcome them.   (IM Cert.)
8 In what ways can marketing planning and control techniques be adopted by non-commercial organisations such as public services?   (IM Dip.)
9 Do you think it is possible to take a miniature of the whole market – a town or a region – and test a marketing scheme

under circumstances which would give a satisfactory impression of whether the scheme would be successful if applied nationally? If you think it is not possible, state your reasons fully. If you think it is possible, what would you look for to ensure that the test area was representative of the whole market?   (LCCI)

10   In what ways could the management of an innovative manufacturing company attempt to minimise the possibility of failure of a new product in the market place?   (IM Cert.)

11   What criteria does the marketer use to determine whether marketing research can help solve a problem?   (IM Cert.)

12   If you are importing a foreign product, what special considerations would you give to the name of the product, its colour, labelling and instructions, packaging, display and advertising?   (LCCI)

13   Suggest some basic criteria which need to be met if a new product is to prove successful.   (IM Cert.)

14   In what circumstances would it be unwise for a company to pursue a policy of innovation?   (IM Cert.)

15   How would you decide the volumes and rates of production of a product in the early stages of product life?   (IM Dip.)

16   How can the establishment of a corporate identity and a corporate image help in the marketing of products or services?   (LCCI)

17   'The price is a signal to the buyer of both cost and quality.' Discuss.   (IM Cert.)

18   What kind of forecasts would you use as an input to your annual marketing plan? How would you conduct them and incorporate them into planning?   (IM Cert.)

19   Describe the main forecasting methods used as a basis for creating the sales budget. Enumerate the strengths and shortcomings of each and show how they can be brought together as a basis for budgeting.   (IM Cert.)

20   Describe some of the special creative advertising and marketing techniques which the mail order trader may use to encourage 'armchair shopping'. Show how these techniques differ from those used to attract consumers to see and buy goods in retail shops.   (LCCI)

21   Describe the main problems faced by a manufacturer attempting to export for the first time and how he can try to overcome them.   (IM Cert.)

22   Describe the principle of franchising and account for the rapid growth of franchise businesses in many countries in recent years.   (IM Cert.)

23 In what ways can sales promotional activities be used to support or encourage the marketing efforts of distributors or dealers? Illustrate your answer with practical examples. (IM Cert.)

24 What are the main advantages in appointing an advertising agency? In what circumstances is it better for a company to set up its own advertising department, creating advertising itself, and placing advertisements direct with the media? (LCCI)

25 It appears that the overall level of advertising is not reduced at a time of recession. How would you account for this? (IM Dip.)

26 What is mean by above-the-line and below-the-line advertising? (LCCI)

27 Services which provide information of various kinds via television receivers in the home or office are now available in many countries. What are the main benefits of such services and who is most likely to use them? How will their introduction affect established information sources such as newspapers? (IM Dip.)

28 How can good or bad packaging make or mar the sales of a product? Describe what you consider to be *five* good or bad examples of packaging which have contributed to sales success or failure. (LCCI)

29 To what extent are theories of personality of practical relevance to marketing? (IM Cert.)

30 Describe the main areas of responsibility of a sales manager, and show briefly the steps you would take to discharge these responsibilities. (IM Cert.)

31 Various forms of after-sales service may be essential if the customer is to be persuaded to buy. State the kinds of after-sales service you would provide for the following products or services:
(i) A sewing machine
(ii) A roof repair service
(iii) Hi-fi equipment
(iv) A department store. (LCCI)

32 Discuss some of the main factors which give rise to changes in consumer needs. (IM Cert.)

33 Who benefits from the introduction of own or private brands? (CAM)

34 What is the thinking behind the appointment of a Brand or Product Manager? In what circumstances would you expect to appoint a Brand Manager and what would be his areas of responsibility? What are the disadvantages? (CAM)

35 What are likely to be the elements of a marketing plan that are the most important to keep control over and why? (IM Dip.)

36 How has marketing activity been affected by the general recession in industrial countries? Can marketing make any contribution to ending the recession? (IM Dip.)

Index